Women in the Hindu Tradition

This book accounts for the origin and evolution of the nature and roles of women within the Hindu belief system. It explains how the idea of the goddess has been derived from Hindu philosophical ideas and texts of codes of conduct and how particular models of conduct for mortal women have been created.

Hindu religious culture correlates philosophical speculation and social imperatives to situate femininity on a continuum from divine to mortal existence. This creates in the Hindu consciousness multiple – often contradictory – images of women, both as wielders and subjects of authority. The conception and evolution of the major Hindu goddesses, placed against the judgements passed by texts of Hindu sacred law on women's nature and duties, illuminate the Hindu discourse on gender, the complexity of which is compounded by the distinctive spirituality of female ascetic poets.

Drawing on a wide range of Sanskrit texts, the author explains how the idea of the goddess has been derived from Hindu philosophical ideas and also from the social roles of women as reflected in, and prescribed by, texts of codes of conduct. She examines the idea of female divinity which gave rise to models of conduct for mortal women. Instead of a one-way order of ideological derivation, the author argues that there is constant traffic between both ways – the notional and the actual feminine.

This book brings together for the first time a wide range of material and offers fresh stimulating interpretations of women in the Hindu tradition.

Mandakranta Bose is Professor Emerita, Institute of Asian Research, University of British Columbia, Canada. Two of her major publications are *Faces of the Feminine in Ancient, Medieval and Modern India* and *Sangitanarayana: A Critical Edition.*

Routledge Hindu Studies Series

Series Editor: Gavin Flood
University of Stirling
Former Series Editor: Francis X. Clooney
SJ, Harvard University

The *Routledge Hindu Studies Series*, in association with the Oxford Centre for Hindu Studies, intends the publication of constructive Hindu theological, philosophical and ethical projects aimed at bringing Hindu traditions into dialogue with contemporary trends in scholarship and contemporary society. The series invites original, high quality, research level work on religion, culture and society of Hindus living in India and abroad. Proposals for annotated translations of important primary sources and studies in the history of the Hindu religious traditions will also be considered.

Epistemologies and the Limitations of Philosophical Inquiry
Doctrine in Mādhva Vedānta
Deepak Sarma

A Hindu Critique of Buddhist Epistemology
Kumarila on perception the 'determination of perception' chapter of Kumarilabhatta's *Slokarvarttika* translation and commentary
John Taber

Samkara's Advaita Vedanta
A way of teaching
Jacqueline Hirst

Attending Kṛṣṇa's Image
Caitanya Vaiṣṇava Mūrti-sevā as devotional truth
Kenneth Russell Valpey

Advaita Vedānta and Vaiṣṇavvism
The philosophy of Madhusūdana Sarasvat
Sanjukta Gupta

Classical Sāṃkhya and Yoga
An Indian metaphysics of experience
Mikel Burley

Self-Surrender (Prapatti) to God in Śrīvaiṣṇavvism
Tamil cats and Sanskrit monkeys
Srilata Raman

The Caitanya Vaiṣṇava Vedānta of Jīva Gosvāmī
When knowledge meets devotion
Ravi M. Gupta

Gender and Narrative in the *Mahābhārata*
Edited by Simon Brodbeck and Brian Black

Yoga in the Modern World
Contemporary perspectives
Edited By Mark Singleton and Jean Byrne

Consciousness in Indian Philosophy
The Advaita doctrine of 'awareness only'
Sthaneshwar Timalsina

Desire and Motivation in Indian Philosophy
Christopher G. Framarin

Women in the Hindu Tradition
Rules, roles and exceptions
Mandakranta Bose

Women in the Hindu Tradition

Rules, roles and exceptions

Mandakranta Bose

Routledge
Taylor & Francis Group
LONDON AND NEW YORK

First published 2010
by Routledge
2 Park Square, Milton Park, Abingdon, Oxon, OX14 4RN

Simultaneously published in the USA and Canada
by Routledge

711 Third Avenue, New York, NY 10017

Routledge is an imprint of the Taylor & Francis Group, an informa business

First issued in paperback 2011

Typeset by
Florence Production Ltd, Stoodleigh, Devon

British Library Cataloguing in Publication Data
A catalogue record for this book is available from the British Library

Library of Congress Cataloging in Publication Data
Bose, Mandakranta, 1938–.
Women in the Hindu tradition: rules, roles, and exceptions/
Mandakranta Bose.
p. cm. – (Routledge Hindu studies series)
Includes bibliographical references and index.
1. Women – Religious aspects – Hinduism. 2. Women in
Hinduism. 3. Goddesses, Hindu. 4. Hinduism – Doctrines.
I. Title.
BL1237.46.B68 2010
294.5082 – dc22 2009024212

ISBN13: 978–0–415–77814–5 (hbk)
ISBN13: 978–0–203–86419–7 (ebk)
ISBN13: 978-0-415-62076-5 (pbk)

To my children
Sarika Priyadarshini and Pablo Shiladitya

yatra nāryas tu pūjyante ramante tatra devatāḥ |
yatraitās tu na pūjyante sarvās tatrāphalāḥ kriyāḥ | |

(*Manusmṛti*, 3.56)

Where women are respected, the deities rejoice there, but where they are not respected, all rituals are fruitless.

Contents

Series editor foreword

Gavin Flood

The Routledge Hindu Studies Series, published in collaboration with the Oxford Centre for Hindu Studies, intends primarily the publication of constructive Hindu theological, philosophical, and ethical projects. The focus is on issues and concerns of relevance to readers interested in Hindu traditions in particular, yet also in the context of a wider range of related religious concerns that matter in today's world. The Series seeks to promote excellent scholarship and, in relation to it, an open and critical conversation among scholars and the wider audience of interested readers. Though contemporary in its purpose, the Series recognizes the importance of retrieving the classic texts and ideas, beliefs and practices, of Hindu traditions, so that the great intellectuals of these traditions may as it were become conversation partners in the conversations of today.

Questions of authority and power are now being asked in relation to the complex field of Hindu Studies and this book addresses some of those questions. While the questions are contemporary the traditions of which the questions are asked go back hundreds of years. Bringing together contemporary issues about gender and power with texts in Sanskrit and vernacular languages, Professor Bose has written an informative, clear account that draws on a depth of learning combined with an awareness of feminist discourse. Examining a range of texts, particularly poetry, from the earliest written records to the nineteenth century, the book shows how women poets in regional languages articulated their aspirations and devotion, and also shows us the official, brahmanical understanding of women as articulated in the law books. While there is little to go on, Professor Bose has done well in bringing out the voices of these women from a past era and showing us the extent to which they were oppressed by the dominant, male discourse and the extent to which they were able to express themselves within those constraints.

Acknowledgements

It gives me great pleasure to begin by acknowledging my debt to my teachers at the University of Calcutta where I began my graduate work studying *Smṛti* and *Mīmāmsā* many decades ago. Professors Pattabhiram Shastri, Heramba Chatterjee Shastri, and Bhutanath Saptatirtha kindled my interest in social thought in the Hindu tradition even though I did not follow their lead at that time. My research effort shifted to the performing arts, to which I remain dedicated, but I never lost interest in the roots of my own world's ethical assumptions and social practice, to which my gurus had shown me the way.

My questioning of the provisions for social living in the past became sharper as I wondered how and to what degree they condition women's lives in our own time. In this I was prompted as much by my own observation of the world around me as by my students in the religious studies programme at the University of British Columbia. Given the wide variety of opinion I have encountered among both the academic and lay public, I began to feel it was imperative to retrieve the formative pronouncements on women, their nature and their roles in the vast intellectual tradition and cultural heritage of the Hindus. For this I made my way back to the *śāstras* of the Hindus that I had studied under my professors in Calcutta, but extended my search beyond these Sanskrit sources to look at texts in several regional languages of India, from ancient to medieval times. The present work reflects that effort.

The preparatory work for this volume was done in Oxford in Trinity Term 2006, when I gave a set of three lectures on women and religion as Shivdasani Fellow at the Oxford Centre for Hindu Studies. I am indebted to the Centre for giving me the opportunity for developing my ideas, especially to Professor Gavin Flood and Shaunaka Rishi Das, but also to the Centre's graduate students. I owe much to Dr Sanjukta Gupta of Oxford for sharing her wisdom with me. It is a pleasure also to thank Dorothea Schaffer, Suzanne Richardson and Emma Davis of Routledge UK, and Jessica Huntley of Florence Production Ltd UK, for seeing the book through publication.

I owe a debt of deep gratitude to the Indian Institute, Oxford, the Bodleian Library, and the University of British Columbia library for the many years of help I have received from them.

Finally, I thank my husband Tirthankar, without whose ever-ready assistance I could not have written this book.

Mandakranta Bose
Vancouver
28 April 2009

The Publishers and the Author gratefully acknowledge the following sources of passages quoted in *Women in the Hindu Tradition*:

Ahitagni, Shivnath, ed. *ṚgVeda Saṃhitā*. Delhi: Naga Prakashaka, 1991 [1904].

Aśvaghoṣa. *The Saundarānanda of Aśvaghoṣa*, ed. E. H. Johnston. Delhi: Motilal Banarsidass, 1975 [1928].

Atharva Veda, ed. and tr. Devi Chand. Delhi: Munshiram Manoharlal, 1990 [1982].

Bṛhaspatismṛti, (reconstructed text), ed. K. V. Aiyangar. Baroda: Gaekwad Oriental Series, no. 85, 1941.

Dehejia, Vidya, ed. *Āṇṭāl and Her Path of Love*. Albany, NY: State University of New York Press, 1990.

Denton, Lynn Teskey. *Female Ascetics in Hinduism*. Albany, NY: State University of New York Press, 2004.

Doniger, Wendy, & Brian K. Smith. *The Laws of Manu*, tr. and annotated. London: Penguin Books, 1991.

Doniger O'Flaherty, Wendy, tr. *The Rig Veda*. London: Penguin Books, 1981.

Grierson, George A., and Lionel D. Barnett, eds. *Lāllā-Vākyāni*. London: Royal Asiatic Society, 1920.

Hart, George L., and Hank Heifetz. *The Four Hundred Songs of War and Wisdom*. New York: Columbia University Press, 1999.

Hawley, John S., and Mark Jurgensmeyer, eds. *Songs of the Saints of India*. New York: Oxford University Press, 1988.

Hawley, John S., and Donna M. Wulff, eds. *The Divine Consort Radha and the Goddesses of India*. Boston, MA: Beacon Press, 1986 [1982].

Ingalls, Daniel H. H. *Sanskrit Poetry*. Cambridge, MA: Harvard University Press, 1979 [1965].

Jackson, William, J. *Vijayanagara Voices*. Burlington, VT: Ashgate, 2005.

Jolly, Julius, tr. *The Minor Law Books*. Part 1. Narada and Brihaspati. *Sacred Books of the East*, ed. F. Max Müller, Vol. 33. Delhi: Motilal Banarsidass, 1988 [reprint of Oxford University Press edition, 1889].

Kinsley, David. *The Sword and the Flute. Kālī and Kṛṣṇa: Dark Vision of the Terrible and the Sublime in Hindu Mythology*. Berkeley, CA: University of California Press, 1975.

——. *Hindu Goddesses*. Berkeley, CA: University of California Press, 1986.

Leslie, Julia. *The Perfect Wife*, tr. of *Strīdharmapaddhati* by Tryambakayajvan. Delhi: Penguin books, 1995 [1989].

Macdonell, A. A. *A Vedic Reader for Students*. Delhi: Oxford University Press, 1993 [1917].

McLean, Malcolm. *Devoted to the Goddess: The Life and Work of Ramprasad*. Albany, NY: State University of New York, 1998.

Miller, Barbara Stoler. *The Gītagovinda of Jayadeva: Love Song of the Dark Lord*, ed. and tr. Barbara Stoler Miller. Delhi: Motilal Banarsidass, 1984 [1977].

——, ed. *Theater of Memory: The Plays of Kālidāsa*. New York: Columbia University Press, 1984.

Olivelle, Patrick. *Dharmasūtras: The Law Codes of Āpastamba, Gautama, Baudhāyana and Vasiṣṭha*, ed. and tr. Patrick Olivelle. Delhi: Motilal Banarsidass, 2000.

Prasad, R. C. *Tulasīdāsa's Shri Ramacaritamanasa*, ed. and tr. R. C. Prasad. Delhi: Motilal Banarsidass, 1999 [1988].

Ramanujan, A. K. *Speaking of Śiva*. London: Penguin, 1973.

Rhys Davids, C. A. F. and K. R. Norman, tr. *Poems of Early Buddhist Nuns (Therīgāthā)*. Oxford: Pali Text Society, 1989.

Roer, E. *Bṛhadārṇyaka Upaniṣad*, ed. E. Roer. Delhi: Bharatiya Kala Prakashan, 2000 [Osnabruck: Biblio Verlag, 1980. Calcutta: Asiatic Society of Bengal, 1849].

Shamasastry, R. *Kauṭilya's Arthaśāstra*, tr. R. Shamasastry. Mysore: Mysore Printing and Publishing House, 1967 [1915].

Sharma, Dipak Kumar, ed. *Durgāsaptaśatī*. Delhi: New Bharatiya Book Corporation, 2000.

Tharu, Susie, and K. Lalitha, eds. *Women Writing in India: 600 B.C. to the Present*. 2 vols. New York: Feminist Press, 1991.

Velankar, H. D., ed. and tr. *Ṛksuktaśatī*. Bombay, Bharatiya Vidya Bhavan, 1972.

Disclaimer

Abbreviations

Āpa.Dh.Sū.	*Āpastamba Dharmasūtra*
AV.	*Artharva Veda*
Bau.Dh.Sū.	*Baudhāyana Dharmasūtra*
Bṛ.Upa.	*Bṛhadāraṇyaka Upaniṣad*
Gau.Dh.Sū.	*Gautama Dharmasūtra*
Mbh	*Mahābhārata*
Rām	*Rāmāyaṇa*
ṚV.	*ṚgVeda*
Strī.Dh.Pa.	*Strīdharmapaddhati*
Va.Dh.Sū.	*Vasiṣṭha Dharmasūtra*
VR.	*Vālmikī Rāmāyaṇa*

1 Introduction

Hindu religious culture correlates philosophical speculation and social imperatives to situate femininity on a continuum from divine to mortal existence. This creates in the Hindu consciousness multiple, often contradictory images of women, at once as wielders and subjects of authority. The conception and evolution of the major Hindu goddesses, placed against the judgements passed by texts of Hindu sacred law on women's nature and roles, illuminate the Hindu discourse on gender, the complexity of which is further compounded by the distinctive spirituality of female ascetic poets.

The wide variety of Hindu beliefs and practices makes it difficult to generalize on most aspects of the Hindu way of life. Given the multiplicity of doctrines and worship rituals, the inseparable interaction of religious and social philosophy, and the continuous accretion of exegetical commentary on all this through several thousand years, it is not surprising that on almost every facet of Hinduism there should be differences of opinion. As soon as one asks, what is Hinduism, one then has to specify which Hinduism and whose Hinduism one is trying to comprehend. There is no doubt that Hindus in general share certain core beliefs and values, such as a belief in the existence of a supreme being independent of time and space, or in rebirth. But whether there is one god or many, whether the supreme being is involved in human life or utterly remote from it, are questions – among innumerable others – that have been fielded with a vast array of answers, many of them subtly argued and equally cogent though contradictory.[1]

Contradictions are particularly common in fields where religious and social ideas intersect or overlap. Not surprisingly, thinking about women, which includes trying to understand women's nature, setting down their rights and responsibilities, as well as determining how men ought to treat women, has proved to be one of the most contentious areas of ethical judgement in Hindu society. Assessing these issues from outside Hindu society has been no less contentious and confusing, especially as external viewpoints, even though they may benefit from the objectivity that distance lends, often run the risk of applying to Hindu ways of life and thought the standards of other philosophical, social and cultural traditions. It is essential to bear in mind that the culture of Hindus is an exceptionally sophisticated tradition of questing after knowledge in the widest imaginable range of human experience, and that it is a quest with methodologies and principles particular to that tradition. Also necessary to note is that despite the growing contact, enriching in some ways, with intellectual traditions from beyond the borders of India, the Hindu tradition has retained its unique character to this day. To begin any study of Hindu culture, then, by listening to voices of historically established authority from within its own ranks seems wise.

Looking for such authority is not without problems. As in all other areas of Hinduism, a grave challenge in trying to grasp the place of women in Hindu thought and conduct is that there is no single body of authority that one might turn to for guidance. Rather, it is necessary to chart one's way through numberless views and precedents towards what may at best be a cautious consensus of informed opinion. This task is a daunting one not only because of the immense volume of research it requires but also because it is constantly at risk of being compromised by the investigator's own preferences – and perhaps prejudices.

Even so, it is both fascinating and necessary to undertake such studies. How may one reconcile the oft-stated prescription for the absolute submission of wives to their husbands with the equally unquestioning adoration of female deities as the embodiments of ultimate power? If the home is judged to be women's ordained sphere, what explains the veneration of women who leave their homes in search of god? Puzzles like these can easily consume a scholar's life. Rightly so, because they are not merely rooted in esoteric philosophy but are also of immediate relevance to social practice. Understandably, scholars tend to probe only small corners of this vast area, and even that has produced a wealth of observations on how Hindus have thought and acted on issues relating to women and how they continue to do so. In doing so, Hindus look for guidance to authorities from the past, but too often only indirectly and through the eyes of commentators from the present. There is a pressing need to pull together the views enshrined in the authoritative texts of the Hindu tradition on a historical basis, and on that basis to construct a textually grounded, general framework within which one may make sense of women's lives in Hindu society. This is the difficult goal aimed at in the present study.

The pursuit of that goal is complicated by the nature of materials we wish to examine. While systems of thought are never independent of social practice, two considerations prevent the present study from turning to social practice as a source: first, the sheer volume of it across time and the multitude of regional traditions put any hope of precisely defined strands of ideas beyond practical reach. Second, distilling ideas from real life practices is an inferential process that may depend heavily upon the scholar's subjective interpretations – or interpretive ability for that matter – and thus stands the risk of compromising its reliability. Works of social or cultural anthropology have been known to be prone to debatable conclusions and to misleading their audiences, even when they are founded on vast surveys, to take Frazer's magisterial work, *The Golden Bough* as one of many examples. Keeping this risk in view, the present work keeps itself firmly tethered to available religious, legal, ethical and literary texts of historically established authority within the Hindu traditional discourse relating to women, with only occasional glances at social customs.

The texts of Hindu law and conduct upon which this book draws are in Sanskrit, the language of elevated thought and scholarly communication in India throughout the centuries-long predominance of Hindu political and social culture, and to some extent even after the decline of Hindu political power first under the Mughal conquerors of India and then under British rule from the eighteenth century till the twentieth. These texts, ranging from the earliest period of written records in India to the nineteenth century, are generally regarded as constituting the foundation of Hindu ideas and ideals. To these we add texts of a very different kind, comprising the poetry and songs composed by women poets in regional languages such as Tamil, Marathi, Bengali and many others, from about the first century C.E. till the seventeenth. These are mostly representations of spiritual quests but also celebrations of secular, human experience. Although they do not primarily engage in disputations on the nature or roles of women, they do complement the treatises in that domain by affirming the independence of the authors from the restrictions of their highly structured society, and at the same time testify to that society's acceptance of their subjective autonomy. Another kind of material cited in this book comes from popular culture centred on domestic rites and regimens related to the worship of a wide range of deities, some local, some mainstream, which are carried out exclusively by women and under women's guidance. Known as *vrata,* these practices aim at securing every kind of success – marital, financial, medical, social – that the family and the home can possibly enjoy. The texts for *vratas* are orally transmitted verses and narratives, and sometimes vary a little in their phrasing from one family to another but not in their basic content. Since the advent of printing in the nineteenth century, the more popular of these texts have been available in print but the oral culture that transmits the rites remains strong. Although on the wane under the conditions of industrial society, *vratas* are still performed and are excellent indicators of the roles that women play and are expected to play within the family.

Admittedly, texts are open to interpretations, no matter how literally one reads them. They are also given to *ex cathedra* or obscure pronouncements often driven by prejudice and partisanship rather than rationality or justice. It is necessary to note here that these pronouncements on women come from men, not women, and as such cannot be taken as free from a gender bias, whether they are sympathetic or adverse to women. Further, one may well question whether a discourse in which women had no part might qualify as representing the entire Hindu faith community. On the other hand, the available discourse does raise essential issues of belief and action and certainly has exerted and continues to exert a distinct shaping influence on women's life – and men's. At any rate, these texts are the best sources we have from a historical point of view, and so, irrespective of whatever sense we choose to make of them, there they are, solidly available to the reader unlike the evanescent images on a computer screen, committed permanently to specific constructions of language. This is why debates over right and wrong, rights and duties, and public and private virtues as they apply to the Hindu identity as a distinct and unique phenomenon have always turned to these texts in search of citable authority in resolving partisan arguments. Hindus are of course not the only people among whom women's issues continue to be divisive but their readiness to rely on past authority is certainly a striking feature of their culture. While one might consider this practice as too heavy and restrictive a dependence on the past, it is in fact an acknowledgement of the continuity of the Hindu intellectual and ethical tradition, which has led to a productive interrogation of a living culture. It is in the hope of participating in such an interrogation that this study utilizes Sanskrit texts from the past as precedents.

These source texts of Hindu belief, from the Vedas or the most ancient sacred books of the Hindus to compendiums of law and everyday conduct, record not only the foundational Hindu conception of matter and spirit but also lay down procedures for earthly existence. This material is supplemented by later commentaries consisting both of exposition and development of the canon, and is illustrated where possible by literary works. The body of opinion thus assembled is organized thematically, for instance, under such categories as attitudes towards the birth of daughters, or women's rights of inheritance, so that we may follow the development of these ideas in Hindu society.

Keeping this general chronological and thematic scheme in view, this book begins with the Hindu conception of the feminine on the plane of divinity, presenting in Chapter 2 descriptions of the major goddesses and some minor ones who occupy the Hindu pantheon or have been part of it in the past. As briefly noted already, the importance of female deities in Hinduism is an intriguing matter. By and large they are powerful figures of benevolence who protect and nurture devotees within a broadly mother–child relationship. But because as protective deities they battle evil, violence is inherent to their nature, which may on occasion erupt into apocalyptic destruction. This ambivalence is usually muted in the conception of Hindu goddesses but it is so potent a subtext in the Hindu view of feminine energy that it demands close attention to the variety and profundity of Hindu goddesses. Giving shape to perceptions of the constituent forces of the cosmos, the Hindu imagination locates the feminine energy at the heart of primordial creativity, which it shapes into anthropomorphic figures of protective authority and compassion. At the same time, it uncovers at the fringes of that constellation of creative energy terrifying impulses of violence, recognizing their destructiveness as an inalienable aspect of power. Far beyond the forceful action that benevolent goddesses take in order to protect humanity and battle evil, as do male deities, the fierce goddesses of Hinduism, often of horrific aspect, wreak havoc indiscriminately with no purpose other than that of wholesale destruction, including cyclic self-destruction. The contemplation of such unbounded and uncontrollable destructive power creates a constant undertow of fear in the construction of goddesses in Hinduism. One may well speculate whether that fear is an acute form of a more deep-laid apprehension of femininity as the location of disorder. But it is also necessary to acknowledge that going well beyond the only too common misogyny that demonizes Woman as Destroyer, Hindu theology situates the destructive forces of the universe in the female persona as embodied in the idea of goddesses of terrifying aspect and irresistible power.

Powerful goddesses are not unknown in many ancient religions, but their survival through several thousand years into modern times is a striking feature of Hindu culture, and their longevity demands close scrutiny because of their continuing and undiminished power to mobilize vast numbers of worshippers irrespective of caste, class and gender. But beyond the historical importance of the survival of goddesses lies their significance in shaping Hindu social thinking about mortal women's roles in human society and the formulation of an ideology of womanly virtue. That ideology, in turn, has given rise as often to literary and artistic representations of women as to expectations from women in their conduct. The chapter on Hindu goddesses will, then, serve as an introduction to the general conception of what the term 'feminine' may mean in the Hindu tradition.

We move from the construction of goddesses to the construction of mortal women in Chapter 3, as it may be derived from the texts of Hindu ethical discourse. Here again the material is vast and it is in this area that we encounter the deepest contradictions within the ethical – and sometimes biological – evaluations of women. That from the earliest times the tradition has never been unanimous but divisive in its views and injunctions, explains why and how later generations of ethicists have succeeded in citing their forerunners as precedents to claim authority for entirely contrary viewpoints. One of the best-known examples of opposite camps citing the same body of scripture is the debate in nineteenth-century Bengal over the admissibility of the remarriage of widows.[2] In more recent times, similar debates with both sides claiming the authority of the past have raged over diverse questions, one of the most distressing being the burning of widows.[3]

These continuing debates over Hindu ideas about the nature, roles, duties and rights of women compel us to scrutinize the sources on which the discussion draws. This chapter attempts to do so by identifying the key issues, under which are gathered the most influential opinions, attitudes and injunctions relating to those issues. This is where opinion swings the wildest. On every matter relating to women, vigorous opinions are set forth, elucidated, expanded, endorsed or contested by successive authors. The merits or otherwise of the views themselves will appear from the material and its exposition presented in this chapter, and these views are not only of historical interest but also of current importance, as we have noted before, in light of the tendency of Hindu society to keep the past alive in the present. But looking past the actual opinions, the discursive tradition they form is in itself worth consideration as a cultural phenomenon. That so much critical energy is expended on women through centuries suggests an extraordinary pre-occupation with women. It is a critical tradition – one that treats its subject as a puzzle so far unsolved but never neglected. Irrespective of the merits or otherwise of the views advanced, one must acknowledge that Hindu thought has never swept the question of women out of sight.

At the same time, though, one troubling aspect of the debate has to be kept in view: who took part in the debate, who shaped it, whose voices do we hear? Women's opinions are conspicuously absent from this vast discourse even though history acknowledges female savants of renown. In the absence of any views they might have expressed, it is difficult not to say that the endless examination of womankind by men within Hindu society is undermined by the fact that it is exclusively by men, unsupported by women's own views of womanhood. Within that long dispute we listen in vain for women's voices. Yet in the larger context of the cultural life of the Hindus, women's voice is by no means unheard, or feeble. The feminine intellectual tradition goes back a very long way indeed, to the discourses in which women philosophers such as Gārgī and Maitreyī took part in Vedic times, but we know what they said only from report. At any rate, these were impersonal debates and reveal nothing about these women other than their scholarly brilliance. But the personal voice is by no means silent, and women's self-representation is a rich treasure-trove, which goes a considerable way back in time and through the medium of poetry and music it forms a substantial body in the cultural heritage of the Hindus. We must acknowledge that the oldest surviving poetry by women is by Buddhist nuns of the sixth century B.C.E.; though not part of the Hindu environment, this incidence of the personal voice of women needs to be noted in the present discussion as a preface to the larger body of women's poetry we encounter from later ages. As Chapter 4 shows by examining the poems and songs by women, these works of personal self-expression is a unique genre if only because they do not participate in the unceasing wrangles of legal and ethical opinion we have noticed above. Instead, through the imagination rather than through formal argument, women poets reach on the one hand for ideas of divinity and the human-divine connection, and on the other, assert their responses to the material world as narratives of personal experience. The nature of women in this body of literature is understood more by implication than exposition. It is not through analytical disputation that we discover how a woman understands herself but through her emotional self-revelation. This self-reflection is necessarily an intense emotional event and expresses itself as poetry and music rather than as academic treatises and revolves around women's personal relationship as much with the life divine as with fellow mortals.

The poetry of women's spirituality in particular is utterly overwhelming in its emotional authority. Transcending social constraints, the women poets of Hinduism find freedom in a direct, unmediated relationship with God, whom they feel, imagine and express in their poetry. That relationship is intensely personal and is expressed through tropes of romantic or filial love. This is not uncommon in the poetry of mystical experience in many cultures, which in India includes both Hindu and Sufi poetry. In adopting these modes and voices the women poets of Hinduism situate themselves within the mainstream idiom of the poetry of religious fervour, at one with male poets such as Kabīr or Sūrdās. To the woman mystic, poetry brings liberation from the constraints of social relations because it gives her a voice which, singing of divinity as it does, cannot be silenced by convention, and which thus lifts her above the gendered constructions of identity prescribed by conventional Hindu thought and practice. This is not to say that these women consciously mount a personal rebellion against the norms of society; it is truer to say that they render the norms set for women utterly irrelevant. That Hindu society has historically responded to such women with reverent acceptance testifies to that society's emotional and intellectual inclusiveness.

In contrast to the inward vision of the women who write of their spiritual states, stands the poetry of women responding to their social climate, which actually predates women's religious poetry. The earliest poetry of this kind is from Tamil literature of the *Cankam* era, which stretched from roughly the first century B.C.E. to the third century C.E. This was a secular literary tradition that included a number of women poets whose poetry opens up a rich vein of responses to human experience of the natural and social world, including love and war. Whether they record the delirious joys of a lovers' union or their anguished pride at the prowess of their warrior husbands and sons, these women respond to their world with an intense passion rising out of a deeply felt personal experience that is nonetheless grounded in public life.

While the women poets of the *Cankam* tradition resonate with contemporary social experience, there are others, from other literary traditions, who find that adjustment difficult. For instance, women in the Telugu folk tradition feel compelled to refashion the conventional ethic of the *Rāmāyaṇa* by viewing it from the base of women's interests.[4] Alternative voices such as these are not at all uncommon though not as widely known or as easily accessible as they should be. In this chapter we shall look at one of the most original of such poets, a woman called Candrāvatī from sixteenth-century Bengal, who wrote a version of the *Rāmāyaṇa* in the voice of its tragic heroine Sītā, in whose suffering the poet sees her own. Underneath her conventional complaint against fate lies a socially mediated realization that women's lives are forever at the mercy of male attitudes, to which she submits but not without underscoring its tyranny. Her surrender is thus a protest against a received order that does not tolerate questioning, and at the cost of her own life's disappointments she undermines the rules women have to obey in a male-dominated culture.

Against the elation one may feel at these women's achievement in casting aside women's customary bondage to social convention, one must set the fact that this achievement comes at the price of opting out of regular social relations. Here again we see Hinduism's ambivalence in thinking about women who are left hanging between deification and subjugation, creating in the Hindu consciousness multiple, often contradictory images of women, at once as holders and subjects of authority. In traditional Hindu society the obvious site for women to exercise any kind or degree of authority is the family, where again we may observe the ambivalence inherent in an individual's exercise of authority solely in the service of the group, often if not usually through self-sacrifice. In Chapter 5 we examine an important area of women's jurisdiction, which involves their control over their own and their family's religious observances. Rather than looking at daily routines of obeisance before family deities as broadly auspicious conduct, the class of observances we shall consider comprises specific purpose-driven *vratas* or rites performed by women or under their direction for the welfare of the family, or, in the case of unmarried girls, for their entry into married, fecund and prosperous family life. These rites, which can vary from very simple and short to extremely elaborate and long procedures, and from personal to collective acts of worship, have appeared at different times to become integral parts of domestic religiosity. They belong so unquestionably to the women's domain that even when their processes demand the services of brahmin priests, the *finale* belongs to women in the form of recitations of the legend valorizing the rite. On contextualizing these *vratas*, then, we cannot help but note once again the multiple roles that a woman is customarily expected to play in the Hindu tradition, at once as subject and authority figure.

The concluding chapter of this study, Chapter 6, therefore reinforces what may seem to be the perplexing argument launched in the introduction, namely that Hinduism does not speak of women with one voice. But this should be no surprise when we note that Hinduism has never organized itself as a unified church with a universal communion conforming to a single body of authorized doctrine. The plurality both of precept and practice has been Hinduism's strength as well as its weakness. Despite the common human instinct for seeking stability in precedent and authority, Hindu thought has thrived on controversy and contradiction, perhaps more so on the subject of women than on any other. It is precisely because the tradition of Hindu thought is so divided on the issue of women that the present study gathers textual testimony from early to recent periods of Hindu social culture, thereby enabling the reader to arrive at an independent understanding of how women have figured in Hindu thought through the ages.

What conclusions may we draw from the injunctions concerning women in Hindu texts of law and conduct, the belief in goddesses and the expression of female spirituality that we examine in this study? As the present discussion repeatedly points out, the opinions surveyed do not allow us to infer any sort of a consensus. What they do and the reason why it is essential that we take note of this enormous variety of opinion is that the historical process of the evolving Hindu discourse on women keeps the subject of women at the centre of Hindu social, cultural and spiritual thought and practice. The scope of this discourse is breathtaking in that it includes every imaginable sphere of activity in which women may be placed and every role that women may assume therein. But it also reaches beyond those spheres by correlating women in the material world with abstractions of the feminine as goddess figures. Women and goddesses are different beings no doubt but in the Hindu imagination they are often conflated on the one hand when goddesses appear as idealizations of feminine virtues and roles and on the other when women appear as vehicles of divine power and authority. This approach humanizes divinity and apotheosizes humanity within a consistent view of existence that takes into account the worlds both of matter and spirit. By doing so, Hindu thought forges links between goddesses and women, and invests women with mystical authority even as it locks them within subservient social roles. That liberating authority and the constraining roles coexist in a paradoxical continuum, which explains how a woman poet embarking upon a spiritual quest is able at once to reject the dictates of her society and to frame her relationship with the deity in terms of familial bonds. It is through such ambiguities and paradoxes that the Hindu tradition projects its conception of women.

Notes

1 For a comprehensive introduction to the Hindu faith, see Flood 1996; for a discussion of the evolution of the idea of the divine female, see Pintchman 1994.
2 See Sarkar and Sarkar c2008.
3 See Hawley 1994; and Bose, 'Satī: The Event and the Ideology', in Bose 2000, pp. 21–32.
4 See Narayana Rao in Richman 1991, pp. 114–36.

2 Gendered divinity

SECTION 1: GODDESSES IN THE HINDU TRADITION*

> While the goddess figure is viewed in the Hindu metaphysical tradition as the active principle of creation and source of all power, she is at the same time defined in familial terms that constrain her within the gender roles prescribed by social norms. This chapter examines the implications of this duality of divinity humanized along gender lines.

Durgā

Kālī

* Unless otherwise indicated, translations are mine.

In the construction of womanhood in the Hindu tradition, the idea of the goddess functions as a philosophical and social archetype. From that archetype models of conduct have emerged to dominate women's lives irrespective of caste, social class and sometimes, even religion. While womanhood and femininity are constructed in the social space, they are also formulated in the metaphysical space, with the figure of the goddess as the common matrix of fabrication. Through time that figure of mystery, grounded in a profound and complex philosophical imagination, has branched into paradigms of mystical, moral and social action. At the heart of the concept of the goddess lies a perception of irresistible energy, which is expressed through action. Abstractions as they are, through time that concept of feminine divinity has become highly complex and goddesses have come to be invested with functional attributes and cast into archetypal roles as:

- mother/nurturer
- wielder of power/protector
- wife/helper/daughter
- destroyer.

Explicated through legend, iconography and ritual, these paradigms cover a wide range of identities, some mutually contradictory in the moral domain, and they continue to be used to define women and to prescribe their roles in life. As Tracy Pintchman usefully reminds us, it is necessary to examine how 'structures pertaining to the Goddess may help shape conceptions of the female gender, the treatment of women in Hindu society, and the roles that women are assigned'.[1] Because of their influence, goddesses are potent and ready sources of images and labels for women in their social relations. In traditional Indian society, the highest respect one can pay a woman is to call her *'devī'*. Barely a step down is the practice of addressing a woman as 'mother'. This usage is of particular value to Hindus and of common currency in India, sometimes extending even to non-Hindus. Whether such terms of exaltation are true indicators of Indian women's actual position in their world is a different matter. On the surface of social interchange, these usages denote reverence, but looking deeper into their social function one may be inclined to see this as yet another mode of marginalization, for a *'devī'* is by definition written out of common human interactions. Those who are familiar with Satyajit Ray's film, *Devī* (1960), based on a powerful story by Prabhat Kumar Mukherjee, may remember how this process can play out in the life of a community.

But a more intriguing conception of the goddess needs to be noted. In traditional Indian society, even powerful goddesses are seldom imagined – just as mortal women are seldom imagined – as single, self-determined persons unattached to a male figure. In Hindu religious thought and practice, particularly in its evolved form, a goddess is always linked to a male figure as his mother or wife or daughter or sister, which suggests that her very identity rests on her relationships with males, with rare exceptions, about which I shall speak later.

At the outset it is important to note that the concept of the Hindu goddess is not static. Between the beginning of the Hindu civilization and today, much imagination and scholarship has gone into formulating the concept of the divine feminine. The numerous images that we view as goddesses are attempts to approximate that abstract conception of a powerful otherworldly being. Here, our first task will be to see in what forms and for what functions these goddesses were imagined by Hindu thinkers, and how their worship has evolved through Vedic, classical, medieval and modern times. These historical periods are of course not dateable to the exact day, and overlap one another by long stretches of time but in general, we think of the Vedic age as stretching from about 1500 B.C.E. to 550 B.C.E., the classical era of the great epics and philosophical and literary works from 550 B.C.E. till about 700 C.E., and the medieval period from 700 to 1700 C.E.[2]

We will begin with the earliest period, the Vedic, and proceed through the rest in sequence. We have to bear in mind, though, that it was in the Vedic and classical eras that the most fundamental developments in the conception of Hindu goddesses took place. Conceptually, medieval and modern times have seen relatively minor changes, which have taken place mainly in worship regimens. However, through the later ages Hindu religiosity gave rise to powerful trends in belief and practice, and continues to do so in our own time, keeping goddess worship at the very centre of Hindu religious life, with deep implications for women's conditions. We will begin our navigation of this complex history by examining the many goddesses that the Hindu imagination has created through the ages, their attributes, their relationships to other divinities, and their place in the Hindu scheme of metaphysical and social existence. We shall then move on to see to what extent the construction of the goddess has proved to be the paradigm for the construction of women in Hindu thought. To keep the line of evolution clear, I shall look at it chronologically.

Who is this goddess? Who created goddesses and how? Does a goddess have an identity of her own? Has she ever been portrayed as an unattached being, an autonomous agent in her own right? In the Vedic era the goddess is situated in the periphery of the divine world, in which she plays an important role but not a central one. For the sages whose thoughts form the ancient Hindu sacred texts, the goddess persona was an embodiment of their conception of the archetypal woman, that is, a parcel of character attributes and functions that were imagined as the essence of femininity, including not only life-affirming attributes but also the potential for destruction. For the most part goddesses were imagined as nurturer, protector, purifier, life-giver, or mother; at the same time, some goddesses were also imagined as malicious or fierce and even malevolent. Given the consistently anthropomorphic derivation of male and female deities in Hindu thought, as in many other religious systems, there can be little doubt that Hindu goddesses were idealizations of mortal women. If so, then behind the Hindu conception of the goddess figure lies an imagination at once reassured by women's perceived life-giving powers and terrified by women's presumed capacity, if not aptitude, for causing harm. That these attributes sometimes coexist in the same persona is a particularly intriguing aspect of this conception of femininity, in that it reflects and at the same time arises from the devotee's simultaneous love and fear towards the object of worship. At some very deep level of the imagination, this ambivalence may well account for the conflicting responses towards women that we shall find in the Hindu texts of law and custom.

That not all goddesses were entirely benevolent was recognized in Hindu thought from the earliest times, as we find in the Vedas. But this line of thinking developed later to include a darker conception of the protective force of goddesses exploding into uncontrolled and indiscriminate destruction. What the Vedas emphasized was the nurturing role of goddesses and their bounty, the principal figures being Uṣas, Pṛthivī, Aditi, Sarasvatī and Vāc. Though worshipped, they were never in the same rank as male divinities. What they meant to the early Hindus and how they evolved – if they did – will be our concern in the following section.

Uṣas

Uṣas, identified with dawn, is the most commonly mentioned figure in Vedic literature and is associated with *ṛta,* the cosmic truth. As an auspicious being she brings light to awaken all creatures but she is also seen as the marker of time. She is the only goddess in the *ṚgVeda* who is invoked in twenty hymns. As Macdonell describes her, 'The personification is but slight, the physical phenomenon always being present to the mind of the poet. Decked in gay attire like a dancer, clothed in light, she appears in the east and unveils her charms.'[3] She rouses all life, sets all things in motion, and sends people to their work (*ṚV.* 1.48.92). She is invoked in prayers to grant long life (*ṚV.* vii.77) and is frequently the sole object of prayers, instead of being included with other deities. Imagined at once as old and young (*ṚV.* iii.61.1), she is thought to be the daughter of the sky who brightens the world. She is sometimes identified as the wife or daughter or sister of the sun but mostly portrayed as a maiden goddess who is nonetheless a nurturing spirit. She drives away the dark forces of the night (*ṚV.* vii.78) and is also called the elder sister of *rātrī* or night (*ṚV.* x.127). This auspicious figure associated with light was lost from post-Vedic literature when new goddesses appeared.

Pṛthivī

Dyāvāpṛthivī or heaven and earth (Dyaus and Pṛthivī) are the most frequently addressed pair of gods and goddesses in the *ṚgVeda*. Pṛthivī seldom appears alone there but assumes a leading role in the *Atharva Veda*. Representing earth, in the *ṚgVeda* she is assigned a supporting role to Dyaus, whose consort she is and with whom she created the world, continuing with him to nurture creatures and plants (*ṚV.* i.159). Gods are also their creation (*ṚV.* i.185). When they come together, the earth is inseminated by the rain they bring (*ṚV.* iv.56). Together they nourish and strengthen *ṛta*, the cosmic law (*ṚV.* i.159). They never grow old. They bestow food and wealth as well as fame. They are not personified, nor do they have any importance in rites of worship. Pṛthivī always appears as a mother figure. Dyaus, a male deity, is associated with the sky but he has less importance in these rituals. He is never addressed alone while Pṛthivī is singled out for direct address in the *Atharva Veda* (*AV.* xii.1) in an entire hymn dedicated to her (*AV.* xii), which portrays her as a great deity in her own right. Addressed as a fertile and nurturing mother, she bestows long life, luck, light and energy to men and women. In later Vedic literature Pṛthivī gains some independence. A marriage vow, *dyauraham pṛthivī tvam* (I am the sky and you are the earth), appears in the *Bṛhadāraṇyaka Upaniṣad* (*Bṛ.U.* iv.4.20), which gives us some idea of how the priests metaphorized the relationship between the sky and the earth. Dyaus, however, remains a minor figure.

Pṛthivī is one of the only two goddesses from the Vedic era, the other being Sarasvatī, who continue to be worshipped to this day. Pṛthivī is known as Bhūdevī and is attached to Viṣṇu in classical mythology. The popular religious tradition of Bengal has a *vrata* (women's special rite), still performed by some women and is called Pṛthivī *vrata*, offering gratitude to mother earth for nurturing humankind. Performed only by unmarried young women, this *vrata* decrees the following prayer:

eso mā pṛthivī boso mā padmapāte ।
śaṅkhacakra gadāpadma dhari dui hāte ।।
khāoābo kṣīr ār mākhan nanī ।
āmi yena hai māgo baḍo rājār rāṇī ।।

O mother earth, come and take your seat on this lotus leaf, holding your conch shell, disc, mace and lotus in your two hands! I shall offer [lit: feed] you thickened milk, butter and cream. May I, Mother, become a great king's queen!

This description links her with Viṣṇu by placing his symbols of divinity in her hands, thereby implying that it is Viṣṇu from whom her power stems. Worshipping her, then, carries the implicit prize of a similar elevation. As Sanjukta Gupta says, 'For women who stay in family life, *vratas* are the most important religious practices for redemption, spiritual elevation and even release from *saṁsāra*.'[4]

Sarasvatī

The Vedic goddess Sarasvatī is associated with a particular river and is praised simultaneously as a goddess and a mighty river. Flowing from her source in the cosmic ocean (*ṚV.* vii.95.1–2), she is full of energy and inexhaustible and on one occasion assisted the Aśvins to restore power and function to Indra's arm.[5] In one hymn she is shown as pervading the tripartite creation, that is, the earth, the atmosphere and celestial regions (*ṚV.* vi.61.11–12). She rules over wealth, nourishment, fecundity, vitality and immortality. She is also called the best of mothers (*ṚV.* ii.41.16) and invoked to protect supplicants. However, her association with motherhood is not given much prominence. In the Vedic cult she is associated with the sacrificial goddesses Iḍā, Bhāratī, Māhī and Hotrā, and is seen as the guardian of the cult. She is identified with purity (*ṚV.* i.3.10), inspiration, eloquence, gracious thoughts, learning, art and music (*ṚV.* i.3.10–12). She is similar to Vāc, another Vedic goddess, and identified with her later in the *Brāhmaṇas*.[6] Goddesses other than Vāc, such as Iḍā and Bhāratī, are also identified with her in the Vedas. She is primarily imagined and portrayed as a virgin, a Kumārī. Early mythology identifies her as the daughter of Brahmā, who desired her incestuously but was spurned by her. However, in a later work, the *Matsya Purāṇa*, Sarasvatī appears as Brahmāṇī, with whom Brahmā committed incest, which is criticized as a sin because she is part of his body (*MatP.* 4). Since both Brahmā and Sarasvatī have swans as their mounts, this establishes another link between them. Yet despite the attribution of illicit congress with Brahmā, Sarasvatī's primary identity is that of a virgin goddess, which has remained constant through time. It is in that identity that she is worshipped today, with her rituals usually performed by brahmins.

Initially a minor deity, Sarasvatī gained importance from the Purāṇic period and assumed a prominent role among the *devīs*. Some later myths identify her as Viṣṇu's wife, particularly in Bengal. As goddesses became more visible and powerful in the later Vedic and brahminic period, Sarasvatī came to assume greater significance. From being the ruling spirit of a river, and thus presiding over the act of purifying ablution, she became the goddess of learning and the arts, this identity being fully established in the Purāṇic period. In a later section we will consider that identity at some length.

Aditi

Aditi, known as the mother of the gods, and also of kings, is associated mainly with motherhood and is mentioned eighty times in the *ṚgVeda*. But unlike Pṛthivī she does not have a male consort in the *ṚgVeda*, possibly because in the Vedic period, as Sukumari Bhattacharji comments, 'the male partner was not considered essential for procreation, so a husband was not thought necessary.'[7] But her role as the mother is always emphasized. Lacking a male consort, she is a free and independent spirit and the guardian of *ṛta*, and is later identified with Pṛthivī in the Brāhmaṇas.[8] Petitioners call upon her to free them from sin and sickness (*ṚV.* ii.27.14). She is best known as the mother of the Ādityas, consisting of a group of seven or eight gods. The list of her sons gradually expanded, additional names appearing in the list through time. An early list of the Ādityas includes the names of Bhaga (*ṚV.* ii.27.1), Mitra (*ṚV.* iii.59), Varuṇa (*ṚV.* viii.25; *TS.* i.5.11), Indra (*ṚV.* vi.59.2), Viṣṇu (*ṚV.* iv.18.4, 5), Aryamān (*ṚV.* ii.1.4), Maruts (*ṚV.* i.172.2), Aṃśa (*ṚV.* ii.27.1), Dakṣa (*ṚV.* x.72.4, 5; v.7), Savitṛ, and Puṣan (*ṚV.* x.85.36). Of these, Mitra, Varuṇa, and Aṃśa are also identified with Agni, and all of them continue to appear in the lists of the Ādityas (*ṚV.* ii.27.1). One of the hymns of the *ṚgVeda* describes

Indra as being nurtured in his mother Aditi's womb for a long time. His birth was very painful to Aditi but after his birth he filled the heaven and the earth with shining brilliance (*ṚV*. iv.18.4, 5), which balanced her suffering and endurance by bringing her the glory of giving birth to so brilliant a son.

Vāc

Vāc is speech. She inspires *ṛsis* and by her help one can aspire to be absorbed into Brahman. She is truth and the vision of immortality (*ṚV*. 10.125), and brings the blessings of language and vision (*ṚV*. 8.89). Although Vāc is identified and absorbed in the idea of Sarasvatī in later Vedic literature, she has a powerful presence in the early Vedic literature in her own right and deserves special mention. She represents sound and speech, *logos*, which control the ritual order. She is associated with Prajāpati and represents *śabdabrahman* (sound representing the absolute) and *sphoṭa* (world created through sound). In this capacity she is the 'word', the sacrificial formula, which brings the cosmos out of chaos into order. Vāc is known as Brahmā's *mānasakanyā* (born out of his mind). In the Brāhmaṇas she appears as a mother figure, creator of three Vedas representing the earth, the atmosphere and the sky.[9] The *Śatatapatha Brāhmaṇa* emphasizes the urge of both Prajāpati and Vāc to create (6.1.2.5–11; 10.5.3.4–12). With her he committed incest, which brought creation into existence. Incest notwithstanding, she holds an exalted position in these texts. In Kinsley's view, 'her role in the *Brāhmaṇas* is suggestive of the nature of *śakti* [primal creative energy] in later Hinduism.'[10] The high degree of her power is evident in the belief that she inspired all goddesses, in the sense of breathing spirit into them.

Śrī/Lakṣmī

One of the most important goddesses, though not one of the earliest, was Śrī, a name frequently mentioned in the later Vedic texts. The name Śrī is often used synonymously with Lakṣmī and it is in this latter name that this goddess continues to be worshipped by Hindus to this day.[11] It is also worth noting, as Bhattacharji does, that the name Śrī and the Latin name Ceres are derived from the same root.[12] Her origin perhaps lies in pre-Vedic Indo-European traditions, but she appears for the first time in Vedic literature, which honours her in a hymn known as the Śrī *sukta*. The term *'śrī'* stands for glory, beauty, prosperity and success, and these boons flow from the goddess Śrī. She possesses many auspicious attributes and functions as the provider of food, the upholder of regal power and noble rank, the bringer of *jyoti* or sacred illumination, prosperity, good fortune, beauty and health (*ṚV*. x.125). As the bringer of wealth to an agrarian people, Śrī/Lakṣmī can also be thought of as an agrarian goddess. Although 'Śrī' and 'Lakṣmī' are interchangeable, the emphasis falls on prosperity when Śrī is invoked and on wealth when it is Lakṣmī. In classical mythology Lakṣmī emerges from the churning of the milk ocean by the gods, signifying the transformation of formless water into organic life. Śrī/Lakṣmī is associated with the lotus, a symbol both of fertility and purity as it grows out of mud but floats above water. Because of this association she is known by the alternative names Padmā and Kamalā, both being derived from synonyms of the lotus. She is also associated with the elephant, which again symbolizes fertility but also royal authority.

Lakṣmī is said to have an elder sister called Alakṣmī, one form of Nirṛti, the reigning spirit of misfortune, obstacles and destruction, who is known as *jyeṣṭhā* and *jāyā*, both words meaning an older woman. In Bhattacharji's view this *jyeṣṭhā* must have been the non-Aryan goddess of prosperity who was replaced by Lakṣmī, the embodiment of Aryan prosperity.[13] In some parts of West Bengal it is customary even today to drive away Alakṣmī before the ritual for welcoming Lakṣmī begins. In many Hindu Bengali households women worship Lakṣmī every Thursday evening but *Alakṣmīvidāya*, the rite of warding off Alakṣmī, takes place only as part of the annual celebration of Lakṣmī in autumn.

An important connotation of the term 'śrī', which occurs frequently in later Vedic literature, is the power to rule and dominate subjects. That power, however, is related more to the office of the ruler than to the ruler himself, and as such she may be attached to anybody who deserves her. For this reason, even though Śrī is imagined as a female, she is positioned in early Hindu theogony impersonally. Through a long period she moves from one deserving consort to another, shifting her attachment to different male figures, such as Soma, Dharma, the two dhārmic demons Bali and Prahlāda, Indra, and finally Viṣṇu as her sixth and final consort. Śrī (prosperity) and Lakṣmī (wealth) are blended into one divinity and she passes from Indra to Viṣṇu.[14] In some legends she is also attached to Kubera but it is Viṣṇu with whom she has resided permanently as a model spouse since about 400 C.E. However, in northern India she is often depicted with Gaṇeśa as her brother rather than with Viṣṇu.

But it is as Viṣṇu's spouse that Śrī/Lakṣmī is celebrated for her constancy in serving him as her lord and for giving up her previous changeability. Her transformation from fickleness to constancy signals a growing need to guard against uncertainty in the world order and to decree stability as the highest social value. It is to underline that need for stability that she is submerged in Viṣṇu to the extent that she incarnates herself as a helpmeet to him whenever he assumes his *avatāra* forms on earth. As a constant spouse she exemplifies orderliness in human relations and society, thus providing a model for human emulation. But we must note that her partnership with Viṣṇu does not necessarily downgrade her for all her devotees. Her independent authority has been so exalted in the *Pañcarātra* school of thought that she is viewed as the supreme object of meditation and worship, in whom are united the cosmic functions of the three great gods, Brahmā, Viṣṇu and Śiva. In a more modest vein the Śrī-Vaiṣṇava school lauds her as the indispensable intermediary between Viṣṇu and his devotees. In general, though, after the Vedic age Lakṣmī has been the defining image of wifely devotion and constancy and the core energy of the stable, prosperous home.

The domestic element is reinforced by the belief held by many that Lakṣmī is one of the many aspects of the Great Mother-Goddess Durgā, whose daughter she is in later mythology, particularly in myths prevalent in eastern India. Earlier myths display some similarities between her and Uṣas, who later faded away, in terms of their beauty. But the similarities go beyond the beauty ascribed to them; both are married to solar gods, Uṣas to the Sun god and Lakṣmī, eventually, to Viṣṇu, also a solar god.

Besides literary accounts, sculptural and numismatic evidence of Śrī/Lakṣmī are found from about second to the twelfth century, showing her hold on the Hindu imagination, which continues to enrich her representation to this day.[15] Śrī appears in relief in Bharhut and Sanchi and the inscription introduces her as Sirimā (in *Prākṛt*).[16] Today, Indian jewellers produce silver and gold coins with Śrī/Lakṣmī carved on one side and either Gaṇeśa or *Om* on the other. These coins are given as gifts on special occasions as blessings.

The annual worship of Lakṣmī is observed on the day of *Dīpāvalī* in most parts of India, except in the Bengali-speaking regions and some other parts of eastern India. There her special ritual day follows the worship of her mother Durgā, on the day of the full moon known as *Kojāgarī Purṇimā*. In Orissa, the festival of Lakṣmī is observed with the distinctive difference that the Lakṣmī-Viṣṇu association is turned into the Rādhā-Kṛṣṇa pairing.[17]

Lakṣmī is one of the most significant figures in Hindu views on women because of the evolution we see in her myth. In the beginning of the myth she is less a person than a package of much-craved social conditions (e.g. prosperity) and personal virtues (authority, nobility). As such she is the standard of a community's high status rather than an individual's aide or property. That is why she keeps relocating from one ruling figure to the other, which suggests that in the beginning of her story she is thought of as the representation of all that is most desirable for a community. Her permanent attachment to Viṣṇu signals the transition of Hindu society to a more authoritarian state in which stability is of the first importance. Tying Śrī/Lakṣmī down to one unchanging relationship achieves that stability. That such a relationship situates her in a position of secondary authority and requires self-abnegation is a consequence of humanizing her within a patriarchal matrix of power. Given the reverence that a goddess is due, it is not difficult to see why she should be a model for earthly women.

Minor benevolent goddesses

A number of other benevolent goddesses were known in the Vedic era but were of less renown and importance. They include Purandhī, Pārendī, Rākā, Dhīṣaṇā and Sinivālī. They bring abundance and material wealth but are infrequently mentioned. Sinivālī, who is specially petitioned for the boon of progeny (*ṚV.* ii.32), appears as Viṣṇu's wife in the *Atharva Veda* (*AV.* viii.46: 3).[18] But her status as a goddess seems marginal and relates her more to humankind, as in the *Atharva Veda* the gods are entreated to implant a male child in her womb:

> *tvaṣṭaḥ śreṣṭhena rūpeṇa asyā nāryā gavīnyoḥ* |
> *pumāṃsaṃ putramā dhehi daśame māsi sutave* | |
>
> (*AV.* v.25: 11)
>
> Almighty Lord, bring forth in the finest form a son in the body of this woman, to be born in the tenth month.

Goddesses associated with Sarasvatī are Iḍā, Bhāratī, Māhī and Hotrā but unlike her they are not related to any river. They are invoked when sacred grass is used during sacrificial rituals. Sarasvatī, however, does not play any important role in sacrificial rituals.

Sūryā, the daughter of the sun god Sūrya, seems to pervade the cosmos and is likened to sacrifice (*ṚV.* x.85.9). Dānu is the mother of the demon Vṛtra and is likened to a cow (*ṚV.* i.32.9). The word *dānu* is also mentioned as heavenly waters.[19] Saraṇyu, the daughter of Tvastṛ and the sister of Viśvarūpa is married to Vivasvat (*ṚV*. x.17.1). She gave birth to the twins, Yama and Yamī, who are believed to be the progenitors of mankind, which provides yet another instance of incest in addition to that between Brahmā and Sarasvatī, and Prajāpati and Vāc. Saramā, known in later literature as the heavenly bitch, does not appear in that form in the *Ṛg Veda*. The goddess Araṇyānī is the mother of the forest, is sweetly fragrant and provides an abundance of food. A beautiful hymn to her occurs in the *ṚgVeda* (*ṚV*. x.146). She reminds us of the *yakṣīs* of later traditions.

Rudrāṇī, Varuṇānī, Agnāyī, Śacī (also known as Indrānī) appear as consorts of Vedic gods such as, Rudra, Varuṇa, Agni and Indra in secondary roles with no independent character of their own. Although the portrayal of these goddesses might be taken to hint that the seed of *śakti* or primal energy is inherent in them, in reality they are minor figures on the margins and manifest hardly any power in the accounts of the early poets, virtually disappearing from later myths.[20] Even so, these goddesses could not have been entirely forgotten because there is a temple of some antiquity dedicated to them near Bhubaneshwar in Orissa.

Spiteful goddesses

Set off against the benevolent goddesses, less benign goddesses form a distinct group in the Vedas. Two important figures conspicuous in their lack of goodwill and occasional malevolence are Niṛṛti and Rātrī. In imagining them the Vedic *ṛsis* (sages) acknowledge the darker forces inherent in the cosmos and invoke them only to keep them at arms length by placating them. Though included in Vedic texts, Niṛṛti and Rātrī fade out of sacred literature in the later, classical period, giving way in classical literature and mythology to fearsome goddesses. Another early goddess was Diti, mother of the *daitya*s or demons, who was not known for her kindly disposition but was not given an important role in cosmic affairs. By contrast, Niṛṛti and Rātrī appear frequently and are habitually associated with gloom and obstacles.

Niṛṛti

Garbed in dark apparel, Niṛṛti represents the dark aspect of the divine feminine as conceived in the Vedic imagination. She rules the southwest quarter of the cosmos where monsters dwell. The *ṚgVeda* dedicates a hymn to her, which paints an unflattering picture of her and urges her to take herself off to some faraway abode, leaving space for benevolent gods and goddesses to appear and bring wealth, happiness and prosperity. Nirṛti is so undesirable a presence that Varuṇa's nostrums are used to expel her (*ṚV*. i.24: 9). She is associated with decay, anger, cowardice, old age and death in one of the hymns (*ṚV*. x.59). Because she was associated with the cult of the dead, the fire altar for her had to be laid in reverse order to the altars at which offerings were to be made to the fathers, that is, ancestors.[21] Through the early Vedic period she grew in power, her sinister side expanding, but later she lost influence. In the Purāṇic period she was identified with Alakṣmī, a goddess who was the exact opposite and elder sister of Lakṣmī, bringer of health, prosperity and happiness. In the *Atharva Veda* Nirṛti appears as the bringer of evil dreams, adversity and ruin (*AV*. vi, 46, 1–2; *AV*. xvi, 5: 4–6). Nirṛti's symbols are many, one being a snake, but a *kapota* or dove is also her symbol (*AV*. vi, 27: 1–3), which relates her to death because several myths link the *kapota* to Yama as his son. As against this, the *kapota* is also connected with Śiva and Pārvatī. Nirṛti is associated with the vulture (*śakuni*) and the ass as well. Iconographically, Nirṛti evokes gruesome associations.[22]

Rātrī

Conceived as the sister of Uṣas, Rātrī appears as a powerful mother figure in her early portrayal, and is endowed with an ambivalent persona, who is both benign and malevolent. She is identified with the night, which provides comfort, rest, security, and is the provider of sleep (*ṚV*. xxxiv.1). By contrast, her negative aspects are underlined by associating her with barrenness and gloom (*ṚV*. i.122: 2; x.172.4). She is associated with the dark powers of the night but is also a protector from their dangers. She also protects her supplicants, providing them with life-sustaining dew (*AV*. xix.48: 1–6), and in collaboration with her sister Uṣas, she gives vital powers to her supplicants (*ṚV*. v.5: 6). When she is with Uṣas she takes on a beautiful appearance and has many positive qualities. The two sisters, Uṣas and Rātrī, light and darkness, are closely related. Metaphorizing the physical world, the early Hindus thought that Rātrī was perpetually followed by Uṣas, and vice versa, thus maintaining the eternal law of creative order and the flow of time.

As we see from this short survey, the female deities conceived in Vedic thought were embodiments of natural forces and phenomena (Uṣas and Rātrī), moral and intellectual essences (Sarasvatī, Vāc and Nirṛti), ritual processes (Bhāratī, Māhī), and family relationships and creative powers (Aditi, Saraṇyu). In this era the community of deities is as yet loosely formed, and in that community the male gods occupy the first rank while the goddesses remain somewhat marginal. Some of them are altogether gone by the later, classical era, new goddesses replacing them, but quite a few survive, some of them merging into one powerful figure. Even then most potent goddesses remain tied to male gods and no matter how powerful in their actions, they are defined by domestic identities. Perhaps the most important development of post-Vedic thought is the emergence of the Great Goddess, a figure of all-encompassing power to nurture and protect all creation and the cosmic order. Absent from the Vedic tradition, she assumes immense importance in later times in the many forms and names in which she is imagined.

The classical age: goddesses of the Purāṇas and epics

In the classical age the idea of the goddess came into greater prominence. New goddesses began to appear from the early common era onwards, often in synthesis with older goddesses. The way they were imagined is particularly intriguing in the context of gender relations. As we have seen earlier, this was the time when the concept of Śrī/Lakṣmī took strong hold of the Hindu imagination, producing one of the most fervently worshipped divinities of all time. Yet, powerful as she is, she is still idealized as the perfect wife. The need for emphasizing the domestication of goddesses seems paramount. A good example is Pārvatī, another goddess who appeared in the classical era. Her myth celebrates her unconditional *pātivrātya,* that is, an absolute dedication to her husband, which is celebrated in legend when, in her form as Satī, she expired on hearing her father speak insultingly of her husband, Śiva. She is not, however, a feeble personality, for she is often identified with Durgā, one of the preeminent deities of Hinduism then and now, who is the epitome of power and bounty. But here again, we find that she derives her energy from the chief gods, all of them male. Male proprietorship does not entirely succeed in the case of Sarasvatī, who survived from the Vedic age as a purifying spirit and was occasionally attached to various male deities, but never for long.

The decline of the Vedic goddesses is balanced in the classical era by the rise of new and enduring goddesses. More importantly, the durability of these goddesses as individuals was matched by the spread of goddess worship as an essential institution of Hindu religious life. Most of these goddesses represent different aspects of *śakti* or primal energy, of which the ideal type is the Mother Goddess Durgā, who has been worshipped since the age of the epics as one who nurtures and protects the universe and destroys its enemies. Related to the conception of Durgā but stretching the Mother Goddess archetype to the utmost limit of protective action was her emanation as Kālī, who in turn came to be surrounded by embodiments of her different aspects. In the beginning, Kālī, this dark goddess of menacing aspect, appears as an unattached figure and is a perplexing being in her terrifying potential for annihilating creation. Associated with her are several other goddesses from this period, namely, Chinnamastā, Tārā and Dhūmāvatī. Related to *tāntric* practices and represented from the beginning as horrific figures, they have remained on the periphery of religious life.

On the other end of the spectrum of attributes stand goddesses distinguished primarily by their tenderness. Two major figures of this time were Sītā and Rādhā, who began as mortal incarnations of Śrī/Lakṣmī. In the beginning of her legend, Sītā was idealized as the perfect wife, the exemplary *pativratā,* and as such a much praised personality but still only a mortal. Time, however, invested her virtue with divinity. Rādhā's apotheosis is more problematic because she does not fit into the common pattern of goddesses, as we shall see, and is valorized on the basis both of *bhakti* (devotion) and *prapatti* (surrender) to one's god. To understand the interrelation between these emerging conceptions of divinity expressed in the female form we will have to look at the goddess figures of this age individually. But first, we must observe the status of one goddess, Sarasvatī, who continued to occupy the religious stage in her own name.

Sarasvatī

Sarasvatī is the only goddess from Vedic times who has retained her importance from that era to this day. She began as a river with the power of cleansing impurity and of bringing fertility.[23] She is associated with speech, poetry, music, culture and learning. She brings wisdom and enlightenment, but also possesses healing powers as a divine physician. Her authority over the faculty of speech is mentioned in the *ṚgVeda*, *Vājasaneyī Saṃhitā*, and *Śatapatha Brāhmaṇa*, while wisdom and learning are mentioned as her province in more than one *gṛhyasūtra*, notably, the *Āśvalāyana* and *Pāraskara*. She is connected with prosperity as well. She appears as the goddess of learning in both major epics of India, the *Rāmāyaṇa* and the *Mahābhārata*, and as the reigning deity of art and music in the *Kāmasūtra* and *Sarasvatīkaṇṭhābharaṇa*. Besides being identified as a physician in *Kathāsaritsāgara*, she is also referred to as the goddess of *nīti* or justice in *Manusmṛti*.[24] If one seeks redemption from the sin of lying, one should offer oblation to the goddess of speech, Sarasvatī (*Manu*, 8.105). In the *Brahmavaivarta Purāṇa* she is associated with intelligence and thought.[25] In many Purāṇas, it is customary to acknowledge in one of the introductory verses the importance of Sarasvatī, as in the *Kālikāpurāṇa*: '*devīm sarasvatīm caiva tato jayam udīrayet* | |' (One should study [ancient] texts [only] after speaking in praise of Devī Sarasvatī).

Unlike many other goddesses, Sarasvatī never acts as an intermediary, for she is an independent goddess who constantly breaks out of occasional linkages with other divine beings, in which she is cast in roles controlled by male figures. For instance, in early literature she is thought to be the daughter of Brahmā and in an incestuous relationship with him. This legend obviously caused discomfort among early writers who tried to find rationalizations. As I have noted earlier, the *Matsya Purāṇa* explains Sarasvatī's involvement with Brahmā, the creator god; it declares by way of excusing the act of incest that creation in the divine mode is different from human procreation. Since there is no physical body involved in divine begetting, the relationship between Sarasvatī and Brahmā, by means of which creation begins, cannot be incestuous (*MatP*. 4.1–6).

Sarasvatī is also thought of as one of Kṛṣṇa's five *śaktis*, that is, aspects of his energy, and co-wife of Viṣṇu with Lakṣmī. In later Hindu thought, Sarasvatī loses her early association with a river and is equated with Vāc, or speech. In that identity she is exalted as *śabdabrahman* and as *mantra* itself. Her sovereignty over wisdom, learning, the arts and music makes her a form of *śakti*. Her annual worship takes place in late January or early February in the eastern part of India, especially in West Bengal and Bihar. Students, teachers, scholars and artists join to celebrate her on a day of festivity. Schools and colleges install large images of Sarasvatī and decorate her for the worship ritual which is performed by a brahmin priest. Her image is immersed in the Ganges or a large tank the next day. Other regions celebrate her in autumn. In Bengali practice she is also worshipped during Durgā pūjā in autumn as one of Durgā's two daughters, the other being Lakṣmī. Sarasvatī represents the *kumārī* or virgin aspect of Durgā. Like other classical goddesses she also is addressed by many names, some of which identify her with *parā* or the ultimate Idea.

Sarasvatī is often depicted with four hands holding a book, a *vīṇā*, a rosary and a water pot. When she is portrayed with two hands (common in West Bengal) she has her book and her *vīṇā*, which establishes her strong connection with knowledge and art. Her complexion is fair (*śveta*) and she sits on a white lotus wearing a white dress and bedecked with white flowers and a swan as her mount. She gives gifts of knowledge and artistic skill to her devotees. Unlike most goddesses she is associated with wisdom rather than fertility and is seen as an independent and *sāttvika* (pure) goddess. In current belief domesticity is not associated with Sarasvatī.

Pārvatī

The dependency relationship between gods and goddesses is nowhere better illustrated than in the case of Pārvatī. She has no independent identity but is defined exclusively by her relationship to Śiva. She first appears as a re-incarnation of Satī, the first wife of Śiva, who dies of grief at his humiliation and thereby causes Śiva to launch a cycle of destruction to avenge her death. It is to dissuade him and to bring him back from his life of renunciation to a worldly one that Pārvatī is born. She is the role model for a Hindu woman in her dedication as a maiden, wife, and later, as mother and model housewife. She is identified with the creative energy of nature, or *prakṛti*. In South India she is believed to be the embodiment of Śiva's grace. Satī or Pārvatī does not appear directly in Vedic texts but develops from Rudrāṇī, the consort of Rudra, who later evolves into Śiva. The *Kena Upaniṣad* mentions Umā Haimavatī as the daughter of Himavat, but she is later identified with Pārvatī, daughter of Himavat. Her role is one of channeling the unbounded energy of Śiva, potentially a destructive force, into the conservation of creation by containing him within the domestic acts of marriage and procreation. This role emphasizes her wifely functions and devotion as well as the physical beauty whereby she lures the ascetic Śiva into a domestic, and therefore an orderly life. This emphasis on the union between Śiva and Pārvatī also facilitates the highly complex issue of the philosophical pairing of *puruṣa* and *prakṛti*.[26]

A brief account of the development of Pārvatī's persona will shed some light on our understanding of how she gradually develops from an ideal wife and mother to take on a protector's role at the same time. The *Yajurveda* associates Rudra (later identified with Śiva) with Ambikā (a prototype of Pārvatī).[27] Pārvatī's benevolence has been a standard aspect of her identity for centuries but in early myths she is associated with Aditi and Nirṛti, making her character rather ambivalent.[28] The vulgate edition of the *Mahābhārata* describes in the *Śāntiparva* and later in the *Anuśāsanaparva* Pārvatī's annoyance at not being invited along with her husband at the *yajña* or sacrificial ritual arranged by her father Dakṣa.[29] The *Rāmāyaṇa* describes Umā as Śiva's wife.[30] As we have seen, Umā is identifiable with Pārvatī, which is borne out by the *Rāmāyaṇa* itself as it later calls Pārvatī Śiva's wife. She is also known as Gaurī because she did penance to become fair-skinned like her husband Śiva. The *Harivaṃśa* describes Pārvatī's penance for winning Śiva as her husband.[31] Her connection with Himavat continues and she resides with her husband and their first-born child Kārtikeya in their mountain abode as the Sacred Family in all Hindu myths. Lakṣmī, Sarasvatī and Gaṇeśa are born later to expand the family, and the holy family of Pārvatī and her children is worshipped in many places in India each autumn. Her domesticity is thus complete.

A vital element of the Śiva-Parvatī myth is their interdependence, graphically denoted by their representation in the Ardhanārīśvara form, which shows Śiva and Pārvatī as two halves of the same body, one male, the other female. This image derives from the amalgamation of the separate cults of Parvatī-Umā-Gaurī and Śiva to reflect the philosophical tenet that the cosmos was born out of the union of the active and passive principles of creation, *puruṣa* and *prakṛti*.[32] Pārvatī is also named as the supreme deity along with Śiva in the same *Anuśāsanaparva* in the *Mahābhārata*. Pārvatī's relationship with Śiva is fully established in its multiple aspects in the classical period. In the *Śaiva-Siddhānta* of the Tamil school of devotion, she is identified as Śiva's grace. In the *Mahānirvāṇa Tantra* she appears as a student of Śiva receiving instructions on a variety of subjects (i.10–13).

In popular belief, Pārvatī is just another name for Umā, Gaurī, Durgā, Jagajjananī, all of which are understood to denote the same Great Goddess. As Wendy Doniger O'Flaherty says, Pārvatī is not only a divinity but *the* Divinity.[33]

Durgā

As a warrior goddess who protects creation from evil, Durgā is the most powerful female figure in the post-Vedic Hindu pantheon. Her birth occurs during a cosmic crisis when creation is threatened by a demon and she arises out of the combined *śaktis* of the major gods with the express purpose of slaying demons. In the *Devīmāhātmya* of *Mārkaṇḍeya Purāṇa* (ch. 81–93) her persona as a demon-slayer, here called Caṇḍī, is vividly described.[34] Conflated with Pārvatī, Durgā becomes Śiva's wife and reigns over a family that is idealized as the model of domesticity. Her familial identity has become a given in popular worship, indeed a prized value, and is celebrated in countless folk legends and songs relating the tenderness of her mother, Menakā, as she thinks of her daughter's life with Śiva, her unconventional son-in-law. Devotees on their part joyously welcome her arrival on earth in autumn as that of a long absent mother and are desolate at her departure for heaven at the end of so brief a sojourn on earth, her paternal home.

But although Durgā is a loving and nurturing mother, she is also a fierce and independent being who needs no help from male gods and acts alone, and if she needs help, she sometimes creates other goddesses out of her own *śakti*. She also defeats those who aspire to dominate her by creating illusions, which earns her the title Mahāmāyā. The *Devīmāhātmya* identifies her with *śakti, māyā* and *prakṛti*, and relates how, after she killed Mahiṣāsura, the buffalo-demon, the gods offered her *stuti* or praise in the litany, *'ya devī sarvabhuteṣu . . .'*, which has become a standard part of the ritual of Durgā Pūjā. Two of the verses exalt her motherly and wifely roles and the rest relate her to *prakṛti* and *māyā*. Ironically, though, even as she is invoked as *māyā*, she remains attached to a male deity, Viṣṇu, when she is addressed as Viṣṇumāyā.[35]

On the other hand, Purāṇas such as *Skanda, Mārkaṇḍeya* and *Devībhāgavata*, and the *tantras* visualize the most powerful manifestations of Durgā as comprising an independent force, thus holding up the alternative model of womanhood found earlier in *smṛti* literature. The goddess in these accounts does not appear as mother, sister, wife or a daughter but as a self-determined divine being in her own right.

Paradoxically in the familial context, she is also celebrated as a virgin. She is known as Kanyākumārī (the virgin daughter) and worshipped under that name at a dedicated site named Kanyākumārīkā at the southernmost tip of India. A special rite for her worship as *kumārī*, or virgin, is known as *kumārīpūjā*, which is part of the evening ritual on the ninth day of *devīpakṣa* (the fortnight dedicated to Devī) of the lunar month in autumn.

That Durgā was originally conceived as a force of nature drawing her powers from the earth is suggested by her early names Haimavatī, the daughter of the mountain Himavat, and Vindhyavāsinī, dweller of the Vindhya mountain. While Durgā's primary role is that of a nurturing mother, that role is sustained by the force of her arms, by her readiness to go into battle, and by her invincible might. In that role of a warlike queen she reveals fierce and terrifying aspects, showing some resemblance to other female deities of destructive potency, such as the early Vedic goddess Nirṛti, the Goddess Caṇḍī of North India, and some of the goddesses of South India. The *Mahābhārata* refers to her as an invincible warrior and mentions rituals and blood-offerings to her by outcastes.[36] Associating her with battle, the *Harivaṃśa* imagines her holding a *triśula* or trident and calls her Triśulinī (*HV*, ii.107.11). Since the Purāṇic age Durgā has been called Siṃhavāhinī because the *siṃha* or lion is her mount, which signifies regal authority and supremacy. She is also associated with other creatures, such as the cow, tiger and dove, but the commonest image of Durgā shows her mounted on a lion, which joins her in subduing and killing the buffalo-demon Mahiṣāsura. Her readiness and ability to destroy her enemies is a vital aspect of her character and links her with her alternate and terrible form as Kālī, as we will see later. It is worth noting that the *Mahābhārata* refers to Durgā as Kālī and Mahākālī (*Mbh*, iv.6.25). But through all the exercise of her might it is her motherly care that shines as her defining quality. Nurturing and energy (*śakti*) are the attributes that have made her the highest goddess in popular estimation, a divinity to whom one can surrender and at whose hands one may seek boons and protection.[37]

At the initial stage of the Hindu tradition, Durgā was not as significant a goddess as she became through the age of the epics and the Purāṇas when she assimilated the powers and qualities of other goddesses and rose to supremacy as the locus of the primal energy known as *ādyāśakti*. The view of her as the embodiment of primal energy became systematized in the *sāṃkhya* school of philosophy, which saw her as *prakṛti*, the essential animating force of creation that complements *puruṣa*, primal matter represented by Śiva, the two together constituting the primordial creative couple. In time, the influence of her cult extended even to Mahāyāna Buddhists who adopted some of the principal deities from the Hindu pantheon, a major example being the *śākta* goddess Tārā, who is conceived in the image of Durgā.

As the supreme female deity in the Hindu pantheon, Durgā is a vastly complex conception that spans extremes of action, from creation through sustenance to annihilation. Hindu thought has essayed to grasp this opposition by imagining as one aspect of this great goddess another divine female of power, Kālī, who is not without compassion but is primarily engaged in destruction. This goddess is one of the most mysterious conceptions in the Hindu tradition and requires close examination.

Kālī

Kālī is Durgā's *alter ego* as her embodied fury. In her propensity for destruction it is possible to see some resemblance to the Vedic goddess

Nirṛti but in the depth, extent and quality of her will to destroy, Kālī goes far beyond. The *Muṇḍaka Upaniṣad* plays on the theme of terror when it identifies Kālī and Karālī as two of the seven tongues of fire (*MU*, i.2.4). In *tāntric* rituals she is another manifestation of Durgā. In the *Mahābhārata* Durgā is identified with Kālī and Mahākālī (*Mbh*, iv.6.25) because of her association with Kāla, or Time. However, she gained such prominence in Hindu thought that she quickly turned into a separate goddess, and although she remained Śiva's spouse, that identity was not emphasized till later. She is fierce to the point of destroying all that she views, an embodiment of annihilation who demolishes every imaginable order as, naked except for a necklace of severed heads and girdle of severed arms, she stands dancing on the supine body of Śiva. According to the *tantras*, *śāktas* believe that Kālī is the 'One', the all pervading energy which manifests itself as the 'Many'. The *Mahānirvāṇa Tantra* describes Kalī in these words:

> *sākārāpi nirākārā māyayā bahurūpiṇī* ।
> *tvam sarvādir anādis tvam kartrī hartrī ca pālikā* ।।
> (*Mahānirvāṇa Tantra*, 4.34)

> Though you have form, you are formless,
> Through your *māyā* you assume many forms,
> You are the beginning of all, but you have no beginning,
> You are the mistress, the destroyer and the preserver.

The earliest references to her are in medieval texts from around the sixth C.E. She is often regarded as a deity in the periphery of Hindu society or in the battlefield. In later times Kālī appears as Śiva's wife but her relationship with him is entirely contrary to that with the other goddesses we have considered so far. Instead of calming him and containing his destructive potential, Kālī incites Śiva in his uncontrolled rage and they feed one another's destructive instincts. One narrative tells of them dancing so wildly that their motion brings creation to the edge of dissolution. In an inversion of the norm of correlating masculinity with violence, most legends tell us that it is Śiva who has to contain Kālī's lust for destruction. In later times two traditions develop in Hinduism, one being *tāntrism* and the other the devotional *śākta* tradition, which was particularly influential in Eastern India. In the first, Kālī represents the ultimate divinity, on whom the devotee meditates in order to gain liberation. In the second, particularly in the eastern *śākta* tradition, the devotee assumes the position of a helpless child who surrenders totally to Kālī as to a loving mother who will reward the devotee with *mokṣa*, or liberation: she is *mokṣadā*, the giver of liberation.

Her emancipatory clemency notwithstanding, Kālī's defining characteristic is her all-destroying fury. She emanates from Durgā to assist her in killing demons such as Śumbha, Niśumbha, Caṇḍa, Muṇḍa, Madhu, Kaiṭabha, and later, Raktabīja. Though she originates in Durgā, she is Durgā's precise antithesis, standing in precise opposition to Durgā's will to create and sustain because of her own will to destroy, even though the two are expressions of the same primal energy. But despite her integral connection with Durgā, Kālī is an independent goddess possessed of a distinctive nature. Violence, even the violence required by justice, is in its very nature a threat to life, and Kālī's violence is so uncontrollable a force that it explodes beyond killing the enemy to universal annihilation. Her apocalyptic slaughter cannot be contained, let alone stopped even by the gods in whose defence she was born. Such is Kālī's power that she may even devour Kāla or time itself, which is why she is called Kālī. Her frenzy of destruction erupts as a wild dance partnered with her consort Śiva, and it brings to the verge of annihilation all creation, which cannot bear the burden of that disruptive energy until Śiva places himself under her feet as a platform to bear the load of her energy.

Obviously, Kālī's theatre of action is a metaphysical location. But as with all products of the imagination, her imagined character and actions do play out on the stage of the human world in a very material sense. What her myth shows is an irresistible force destroying all structure, order and life in a paroxysm of gruesome violence, purportedly on the spiritual plane. Transported to the earthly plane of human life, this means that Kālī stands for all that might conceivably disrupt the controlled social order of brahminic dispensation. Though she emanates from Durgā, Kālī's independence from all attachments designates her as an outsider. As such she is a constant threat to social order and so, in her early myth, she is located outside human habitation, residing in cremation sites in the company of lost spirits.

At its inception, then, Kālī's portrayal primarily acknowledges the terror and the unease of devotees used to the character profile of the divine benefactress. Clearly, Hindu thought was caught in a dilemma: this terrible goddess had to be invested on the one hand with the power to annihilate evil, and on the other, mercy for the good and the just. What was needed was a control mechanism, some device to bring her within the stable order of human society, in other words, to tame her, to tie this wild female down to some semblance of the life of ordinary mortals. This was best done by domesticating her, by bringing her in from the battlefields and cremation sites, by making her the wife of Śiva – one might say, Pārvatī in another guise. As a turbulent spirit Kālī was a fit spouse for Śiva, himself something of an outsider in the community of gods, and both have continued through the history of Hindu belief to be associated with secret sites and magic rites. Nevertheless, from the late classical age on, the response to Kālī ceases to be fear alone and she begins to be located within city temples and family homes. In time, familiarity on the one hand and fascination with power on the other combine to transform this once dreaded divinity into a mother figure of wild beauty and compassion. She is no longer remote, and her liberating action takes place here and now, granting deliverance in this world, even before death.[38] This trustful intimacy between the goddess and her devotee is effected by *bhakti*, that is, the spiritual way of ecstatic devotion to one's deity. This sense of union stretches even to the devotee imagining the goddess as his daughter, a young girl of infinite grace and love. The goddess is commonly addressed as Mother. But Rāmakṛṣṇa Paramahaṃsadeva, a charismatic nineteenth-century devotee of Kāḷī, saw her both as his mother and daughter. Thus, from a figure of menace Kālī becomes one of reassurance, the marginal becomes central, and the dance of death becomes the beat of life. Philosophically as much as emotionally, no inversion could be more radical.

This transfiguration occurs by means of compelling visual and linguistic processes in the treatment of Kālī's appearance. As I have remarked before, terror is inscribed in her body: she is black-skinned, attired only in human body parts, her hair flying and her red tongue hanging out to lick up the blood of her enemies. Yet in the devotee's eye her dark skin glows with light, her hair dances to cosmic rhythm, and her face radiates grace. In the higher understanding claimed by the devotee, the grotesque is not grotesque but beauty itself and black is not black but some ineffable radiance. The best known *śākta* poet of eastern India, the eighteenth-century Bengali author Ramprasad Sen, says, '*śyāmā mā kī āmār kālo re*' (Who says my mother Śyāmā is dark?), converting the stigma of blackness into a blazon of glory. A powerful linguistic strategy that mediates the softening of the coloration is the use of the name Śyāmā in preference to Kālī, for it is derived from 'śyām', a word idiomatically tied to the composite imagery of the soft hue of a youthful body shimmering with the flush of the green earth. Thus transformed, Kālī has revolutionized the Hindu idea of the divine female.

Tantra and goddess worship

From the Purāṇic period onwards goddess worship came to occupy a very prominent place in the Hindu tradition. The goddess, in the imagination of early as well as subsequent thinkers of the tradition, has remained an ambivalent figure, portrayed both as a benevolent and a malevolent being. Her mystery deepened in the Purāṇic era when a new tradition of religious philosophy and practice arose. Known as *tantra* and gaining great strength through the ages well into the beginning of the twentieth century, it is a path of esoteric principles and occult rites. Since *tāntrism* regards *śakti* as the quintessence of divinity (*Śaktisaṅgama Tantra,* 2.13.44), it is grounded in the worship of *śakti,* holding at its centre the idea of the goddess, whose material form it identifies as mortal women to the point of equating them with the goddess (*Durgāsaptaśatī,* 6.2).

Between the fifth and the eleventh century, the tradition of *śākta tāntrism* produced a number of texts that describe two types of goddess, ŚrīKula and KālīKula, benevolent and terrifying. ŚrīKula texts, known as Śrī Vidyā, centre on the worship of Lalitā Tripurasundarī which developed in South India, whereas KālīKula texts expound the cults of Kālī, which can be traced back to Kashmiri Śaivism from the seventh and eighth centuries. The difference between these goddesses is significant. Lalitā Tripurasundarī is believed to be the *tāntric* form of Lakṣmī and is worshipped in the form of a *yantra* or magic diagram, and to the chanting of a fifteen syllable *mantra*. *Lalitasahasranāmā*, *Saundaryalaharī* and *Tripura Upaniṣad* are prominent treatises in praise of this form of *śakti*.[39] The goddess in the ŚrīKula tradition is conceived as an impersonal power, distant from the worshipper. The texts of the KālīKula school, such as the *Jayadrathamālā* and *Kubjikātantra* reflect cults developed in the northern and eastern area which regard Kālī as the light of pure consciousness and the absolute power of the universe who stands even above Śiva Bhairava.[40]

The advent of *tāntrism* brought important shifts in goddess worship. Not only did it make goddess worship pre-eminent in Hindu religious life, it also expanded the pantheon of goddesses and the idea of the goddess in line with *tāntric* philosophy. While brahminic religion remained the mainstream tradition and the major goddesses from Vedic and Purāṇic times survived within it, some of their attributes were reconfigured to emphasize the *tāntric* concepts in thinking about goddesses. This reformulation of the goddess was not a complete break from the past, for some of the attributes of goddesses in *tāntric* thought overlapped with those of the earlier figures. To put a highly complex idea simply, *tāntrism* asserted that *śakti* or primal energy was at the core of all phenomena, spiritual, intellectual and material, the only reality, and that the supreme manifestation of *śakti* was the divine female in her variety of forms. Nonetheless, the numerous forms of devī, the generic term for goddess, can be separately identified, as we shall see in the quick survey here.

Mahādevī

The central figure in the *tantra* view of divinity is Mahādevī, or Devī, who is a powerful, creative, active and transcendent female divinity. All other goddesses, including Pārvatī, Durgā, and Lakṣmī, are understood to be aspects of Devī. In many texts she is described as the supreme and unmatched ruler of the world and its root. She is the mother of all, the life force in all beings, and the sole cause of the universe. According to the *Devī Bhāgavatapurāṇa*, she is the creator of Brahmā, Viṣṇu and Śiva, and commands them to carry out their cosmic tasks. Four crucial philosophical ideas animate the concept of Mahādevī, namely, *śakti, prakṛti, māyā* and *brahman*. Impalpable even to spiritual vision and expressing herself as the basic matter of the universe through illusory perceptions, she is not merely the essence of energy but transcendent reality. Conceived as the ultimate divinity, she is a distant, awe-inspiring figure but one who is always responsive to the pleas of her devotees. She cannot be bounded by particular attributes and from her emanate many female deities, all of them forceful beings and some of them violent.

Mātṛkās and Mahāvidyās

The following types of goddesses, the Mātṛkās and Mahāvidyās, are given to violence and are not widely worshipped.

Mātṛkās

The Mātṛkās, or the Mothers, comprise an extremely important group of goddesses who are clearly understood not to be divine consorts or *śaktis* of male deities but are extensions or forms of Devī herself. They are primarily an independent group of goddesses possessing a violent nature and are associated with diseases, particularly those affecting children. Matṛkās appear in various Purāṇas, the best known account appearing in *Devī Māhātmya*.

The Mahāvidyās

The Mahāvidyās are a distinct category comprising ten goddesses, namely, Kālī, Tārā, Chinnamastā, Bhuvaneśvarī, Bagalā, Dhūmāvatī, Kamalā, Soḍaśī, Mātaṅgī, and Bhairavī. Their fearsome traits are derived from Nirṛti, although that Vedic goddess has faded away from common belief by the time the *tāntric* deities appear. They were born out of Satī's anger at being denied an invitation to her father Dakṣa's *yajña* because of his contempt for her husband Śiva. Excepting Kamalā and Soḍaśī, who express the eternally youthful energy of Devī, the Mahāvidyās are terrifying beings who represent her violent and destructive aspects.

The appearance of these goddesses and the general spread of goddess worship were not the only important milestones in the history of the Hindu belief system. Other major developments were the deification of mortals – especially Sītā and Rādhā – and the emergence of local deities. Local goddesses were regarded as the ruling deities of particular villages or specifically consecrated sites, with their influence limited to their immediate environs. These goddesses were compounded of the traits both of *tāntric* and classical goddesses but were also invested with attributes that answered to the historical, cultural and material experience of their localities. In conception they were relatively simple as representations of natural phenomena and responses to local needs, which often shaped them as terrifying goddesses who had to be placated and worshipped to ensure peace and prosperity locally. Sītā and Rādhā, on the other hand, were idealizations of the highest life-affirming traits attributable to women. Thus, their relevance to women's lives could be hardly overestimated.

Sītā and Rādhā: from human to divine

Unlike the goddesses discussed so far, Sītā and Rādhā were born mortals but later elevated into the list of goddesses. Both are seen as incarnations of Lakṣmī while their partners, Sītā's husband Rāma and Rādhā's divine lover Kṛṣṇa are regarded as *avatāras* or incarnations of Viṣṇu, as emphasized in epic and Purāṇic texts. Given the background of both Sītā and Rādhā as women whose lives revolved exclusively around their male partners, they are understandably held up as role models for Indian women. For most devout Hindus Sītā remains the epitome of Indian womanhood as a totally voiceless, selfless, submissive and devoted wife. This may not entirely agree with the original version of her legend, as her portrayal by *ādikavi* (First Poet) Vālmikī in his *Rāmāyaṇa* shows, but that is the image in which she is revered by the vast majority of Hindus and the reason for her apotheosis. In light of the ideological pressures of a patriarchal society the adoration of Sītā is not hard to understand. On the contrary, Rādhā's deification is most puzzling, as her conduct as a married woman taking a lover violates every norm of the social order. However, in the *bhakti* mode of defining the relationship between the deity and humankind, the highest human joy – and duty – is to give oneself to one's god, social obligations notwithstanding. That is of course what Rādhā does, transgressing against marital and family duties in the face of social censure. She is thus transformed from an erring wife into a role model of devotion and submission. These models call for a closer look because of their abiding influence on women's lives from medieval to modern times.

Sītā

Sītā is perhaps the most popular heroine of Hindu mythology. As Rāma's ever-devoted wife she sets the pattern for wifely behaviour by remaining uncomplainingly loyal to her husband despite suffering injustice at his hand. In fact, in the original story by Vālmīki she is not quite so meek, as several recent studies have demonstrated,[41] but it is by meek dependency that later tellers of the *Rāmāyaṇa* came to define her, excising her self-asserting dignity from her legend. It is useful to note that the name Sītā predates the character in the *Rāmāyaṇa*. A goddess of that name appears in Vedic literature as a fertility figure, which is consistent with the meaning of the term *sītā* or furrow.[42] She is also attached to various gods during this early period. But Sītā as a fully developed character blossoms in the epic *Rāmāyaṇa* and forever remains the faithful and devoted wife of Rāma. Although in the *Vālmikī Rāmāyaṇa*, she is recognized as an incarnation of Lakṣmī,[43] the emphasis is on her human identity, not a goddess on earth. Her deification was a late development that occurred through regional versions of the *Rāmāyaṇa*. Interestingly, though Sītā was turned into a devī, her countless devotees do not think of her as an embodiment of power,[44] but rather as a submissive and docile wife.[45] In today's India, specially in northern India, Tulasī's *Rāmcaritmānas* has become the most influential Rāma story, and public perception of the narrative and its characters is now dominated by the TV version produced by Ramanand Sagar in 1987 following Tulasī, further reinforcing the submissive role of Sītā.[46] In this North Indian version, Sītā blames her fate on herself, saying that she must have done something wrong in either this or her previous life which brings her suffering. She never blames Rāma but herself. In this version, Sītā has a secondary role as a devotee who acts as an intermediary between Rāma the god and his followers. In this role, although she is a goddess, she does not hold as high a position as Rāma does and remains in a subordinate position in relation to God Rāma.

Given the focus on gender in this book, it is worth pointing out that contrary to popular belief, Sītā is a woman of great strength in the original source. It is possible to view her tragedy as a series of sacrifices she makes for the common good. It is her own decision to accompany Rāma into exile in the forest (*VR*. ii.26) right at the beginning of the story. The decision to go through the fire-ordeal Rāma requires after her rescue as proof of her chastity is again her own, voicing an impassioned protest at her humiliation (*VR*. vi.117–119). Finally, at the end of the story, after her final banishment as it is told in the *Vālmīki Rāmāyaṇa*, it is she who decides to end her life by turning away from Rāma to seek sanctuary with her mother, Goddess Earth. Throughout her life Sītā never accepts injustice without protest, even registering her scorn for what she calls Rāma's *prākṛta* (ignoble) conduct in doubting her chastity and advising her to attach herself to another male.[47] Against this original representation of Sītā as a powerful personality, she has come to comfort the hearts of devout Hindus as the voiceless and submissive wife and the epitome of Indian womanhood and remains so.[48] This ideal was constructed by post-Vālmīki authors, whose manipulation of the story advances a particular view of women's place in society. Such is the potency of that ideal that it has traditionally succeeded in securing women's willing consent to subjugation.

Rādhā

In contrast to Sītā, Rādhā is a surprising nominee for apotheosis. She has not the faintest claim to divinity at the beginning of her legend for she is no more than a human heroine in an adulterous relationship (she is *parakīyā*, married to another man) with a man half her age who is socially related to her. Her deification despite this otherwise censurable situation paradoxically elevates her to divinity because the object of her love is the god Kṛṣṇa. This transmutes her offence into the highest virtue, that of desiring union with the godhead. Interpreted not socially but metaphysically, her yearning for Kṛṣṇa makes her a symbol of humanity's total, unconditional and selfless surrender to the ultimate godhead.

The Rādhā–Kṛṣṇa love story began as a human romance but in the Purāṇic era that story developed into an allegory of the human-divine relationship. The *Vāyu, Matsya and Varāha* Purāṇas mention Rādhā but it is in the *Devībhāgavata, Brahmavaivarta* and *Padmapurāṇa* that she is described at length. Theses texts reveal Rādhā as the complement to Kṛṣṇa and therefore a divine being. Early legends accord her little importance beyond counting her merely as one of the *gopīs* or cowgirls but the later Purāṇas, such as the *Brahmavaivartapurāṇa*, acknowledge her as an aspect of Devī, more specifically as Kṛṣṇa's *śakti*. Her elevation is complete when at one point she is identified with Lakṣmī.

Rādhā's deification has been problematic for some devotees who find it difficult to come to terms with an unsanctioned relationship. The Vallabha *sampradāya*, for instance, portrays her as Kṛṣṇa's wife in order to justify their relationship. Vaiṣṇavas on their part think of Kṛṣṇa as the only male in the cosmos because he is the Creator. As a result of this belief, Vaiṣṇavas, both male and female, see themselves as Rādhā in relation to Kṛṣṇa. An example of this transforming devotion was Śrī Caitanyadeva, the fifteenth-century spiritual leader of the Vaiṣṇavas who aspired to union with Kṛṣṇa as Rādhā. Today, most devotees accept Rādhā and Kṛṣṇa as transcendental lovers and not as a married couple.[49] On the social plane Vaiṣṇavas understand Rādhā's love as the ultimate type of selfless attachment because she sacrifices her reputation by rejecting social norms. On the metaphysical register, Vaiṣṇavas, particularly those of the Bengali tradition, take her love as a potent metaphor of the human yearning for the divine.

Because Rādhā's love is at once intense and illicit, it has been a magnet for poets and artists. Her pining for Kṛṣṇa appears in early writings by Hāla (early common era), Bhaṭṭanārāyaṇa (prior to eighth century C.E.), Vākpati (seventh–eighth century), Ānandavardhana (mid-ninth century), Abhinavagupta (tenth century), Rājaśekhara (ninth–tenthth century), Kṣemendra (eleventh century) and Hemacandra (eleventh–twelfth century).[50] But perhaps the most brilliant celebration of the Rādhā-Kṛṣṇa theme appears in the twelfth-century poet Jayadeva's *Gītagovinda*. This long poem in several parts portrays the culmination of their love in the romantic idiom of love poetry but views it allegorically as the human soul's spiritual union with the ultimate being. Jayadeva identifies her with Śrī (i.2; i.23) and Lakṣmī (xi.22), and Kṛṣṇa as an incarnation of Viṣṇu. Jayadeva's Rādhā is tormented by *viraha* or love in separation. Her world-forsaking urge to be with him compels her to follow him as an *abhisārikā* (a woman who goes to meet her lover ignoring social censure), travelling along hazardous forest paths at night oblivious to reproaches by her husband's family.

Vidyāpati and Caṇḍīdās (both from around the fourteenth to fifteenth centuries) commemorate Rādhā's illicit love as the apex of romantic passion, exalting her unflinching resolve to stand up against the entire world. That despite this revolutionary character of her love Rādhā is passionately adored suggests the feminization of spirituality, which centralizes the female as the locus of mystic energy. This might seem another strand in the spread of goddess worship under *tāntrism*, except that here the perception of female divinity occurs not through occultism but by idealizing the man–woman relationship as allegorical truth.

How may one compare Rādhā with Sītā? How could two such different women be adored as goddesses? Most of those who know the *Rāmāyaṇa* regard Sītā as the perfect example of the uncomplaining wife whose sole purpose in life is to follow her husband's every wish and to put his interests above her own. Clearly, Sītā places her allegiance to duty above personal interest.[51] Undoubtedly, her love for Rāma is a deep emotional feeling but that is not an issue in the foreground of her fame. Her society and ours regard her love as her duty, and approve the fact that in fulfilling that duty she plays the role of wife exactly as expected by society. She is praised for her sustained *tyāga*, that is, renunciation of personal benefit and comfort for duty's sake.

A degree of irony enters into our comparison when we talk about renunciation: Rādhā too is a renunciate, but in quite the opposite sense. While Sītā renounces her personal interests in favour of social and familial duties, it is precisely those duties that Rādhā renounces in pursuit of her personal choice. Rādhā throws aside exactly the bonds that Sītā accepts and receives no blame for what would be an unthinkable transgression in any other woman, including Sītā. Sītā bows to a life of suffering entirely because she puts public good above the private. Yet both are equally selfless, equally ready to sacrifice all in the service of a higher goal, except that Sītā's goal is determined by social expectations and Rādhā's by their rejection.

Sītā and Rādhā are very different characters and follow very different paths in forging links with their divine partners. But to their devotees they tower above common mortals by virtue of the force of their resolve, which demands the adoration due to the goddess persona characterized in Hindu thought by an inalienable ownership of primal energy. Under that condition, the deification of neither human heroine should be surprising. What is undoubtedly surprising is that both Sītā and Rādhā are worshipped with their male consorts and never alone, no matter that they are goddesses. There is no temple that I know of dedicated to either of them where they are worshipped in their own right. Female dependency holds as true for goddesses as for ordinary women.

Village goddesses

With village goddesses we step into a less speculative realm of spiritual reasoning and practice. These goddesses are as numerous as the villages of India in which the majority of India's population still resides. These villages tend to have their own resident divinities, of whom most are goddesses. The instinct and logic underlying faith in them are clear matters of give-and-take. They protect villages from mishaps and ensure timely rain, good crops and good health. They are also directly connected with disasters both as inflictors and protectors. For these reasons their conception and worship revolve more around the practical motive of keeping them contented than spiritual attachment, although the latter cannot be discounted for every worshipper, nor for every individual divinity.

As embodiments of basic natural forces, village goddesses are usually not represented by anthropomorphic images but as plain rocks, trees or small shrines that contain no images. Seldom associated with a male deity, village goddesses are thought to predate the founding of their respective villages or to have actually founded their villages, and the villages themselves are usually considered to be the consorts of the goddesses in place of male divinities. In view of this relationship, the entire village, no member excepted, worships as an indivisible body because the good or evil of one involves that of all, and vice versa. It is, after all, a local matter. Benevolent and malevolent goddesses alike are appeased and entreated to ensure happiness and health. They are independent goddesses and are not considered as role models for ordinary women. However, unlike mainstream goddesses who are dangerous and menacing when they are independent and unmarried, a village goddess ensures order, calm and stability in her own village, which she protects when appeased.[52]

Most village goddesses are unknown beyond their own locations but some exert influence well beyond their immediate environs or even a particular region. Two major goddesses of wide renown and power are Manasā and Śītalā. Both of them are feared for the disasters they may visit on the unbeliever. Manasā, the goddess of *nāgas* or snakes can cause death and disorder if not appeased. She remains popular in northern and eastern India and in the monsoon months of July and August *(śrāvaṇa* and *bhādra),* when snakes appear most frequently, women send milk and banana to her temple. The other feared goddess is Śītalā, who is the goddess of smallpox in northern India, with a counterpart in southern India called Māriyāmman. Typically and logically, it is during the spring months when the incidence of small pox is the widest that she is most fervently worshipped by devotees who look to her for blessings as a prophylactic against the disease.

This survey must also include the North Indian goddess Santoṣī Mā who is a more recent addition to the pantheon of goddesses. First heard of in the 1960s, she became hugely important after her legend was presented in a Hindi film in 1975. Through the past three decades she has become a pan-Indian goddess claimed to be the Ultimate Spirit, Mahādevī in person, and is worshipped by a large number of women. In worshipping her, brahminical rituals are performed side by side with festivities from folk practice. Similarly modern is the surge of devotional interest in several other regional goddesses, for instance, Māriyāmman or Aiyāppan in South India. Peripheral to begin with, these goddesses have been raised to the Pan-Hindu consciousness through the Sanskritization of their rites and myths, that is, by the use of the Sanskrit language in their worship and by their inclusion in traditional Hindu myths whereby they have been projected as manifestations of Devī, especially Durgā.

Although the story of Hindu goddesses is a complex one, it is possible to generalize, as many students of Hindu thought have done, that they fall into two broad categories of identity. Gavin Flood observes in his *Introduction to Hinduism* that 'there are two kinds of goddess representations: a ferocious form such as Kālī, and a gentle, benevolent form such as Tripurāsundarī or Lakṣmī.' [53] David Kinsley differs from many scholars of Hinduism when he denies that Hindu divinities are forms of a fundamentally unified conception of the godhead. But he accepts the common classification of Hindu goddesses into two broad categories, one characterized by the maternal instinct, the other by the submerging of that instinct in their destructive will, even though they may be addressed as 'Mother', which is more a form of respect, as we have seen, rather than a signifier of function. The implications of this division for women's lives and society's expectations from them are enormous, for, as I suggested in the beginning, it is from the perceived identities of goddesses that models of conduct for women are drawn. Respect and approval are won by the woman who acts as a self-sacrificing wife or mother who is also self-effacing except when energetic action is required to protect her family. At the same time, the process may also be seen in reverse inasmuch as socially desirable characteristics of women are imputed to goddesses and thus valorized, which in turn enforces the assumption of such traits by mortal women.

The type of goddess marked by benevolence has given rise to the most influential models for women, all designed to inspire devotion to domestic functions, from women's self-preparation for marriage, to loyalty to the husband, to nurturing children, and conserving the family's well-being. Pārvatī is the exemplar of unrelenting efforts to become a suitable bride. The legend of Lakṣmī provides the pattern of the wholly devoted wife and of the compliant bride within the system of arranged marriages. Durgā is revered as the protector of her children and though her wrath is not exactly enjoined upon the earthly mother, it is implicit in the expectation that a mother must go to all lengths to save her children from harm. The translation of these goddesses into human role models shows the requirements of social order very plainly indeed, especially in the weakening of emphasis on the power inherent in the Great Goddess persona of Durgā. Given the 'paramount importance of the roles of wife and mother for Hindu women', that Samjukta Gupta speaks of,[54] it has been the practice not to draw too much attention to the goddess as a transcendental force. Hence, it is the loving aspect of these goddesses that is emphasized, and their roles as wives and mothers that are held up for imitation. This focus on familial roles explains the popularity of Sītā, who, as the idealized wife born as a mortal but carrying the sanctity of her divine origin, bridges the gap between the divine and the human, softening the element of power implicit in the divine persona into the tenderness of the wife.

Before I move on to the other category of fierce and destructive goddesses, let me note that between the two polar identities there is an area in which alternative models for women may be generated. Indeed, this seems to me a particularly sophisticated aspect of Hindu thought on femininity, for it acknowledges that there is a part of female nature which resists conventional social roles without subverting them. This acknowledgment centres on Sarasvatī, the one goddess who refuses to be bound to the service of male figures. As a female being without husband or children, Sarasvatī pursues an independent existence on a plane elevated from mundane family life or common social relations. Thus, for the rare mortal female who renounces ordinary worldly life or is forced to forego its pleasures and demands, Sarasvatī is a viable model within the order of conventional society.

The ferocious beings imagined as deities of destruction, necessary as such destruction may be, are obviously not models for women. How, then, may they be relevant to the Hindu idea of womanhood? Before considering this I must remind the reader that Kālī or the still more fearsome Chinnamastā or Cāmuṇḍā are not uniformly and entirely dealers in death and destruction but also benevolent and munificent to their devotees. Even in their rage they can be stopped by sincere supplicants. Besides, their rage is in fact a response to the need for protecting their supplicants. That is why, on considering Kālī's history in the Hindu imagination, it is impossible to miss a deep anxiety, for she is at once essential to the survival of the universe and a threat to it. The response to this anxiety is twofold: she is either pushed to the periphery of social space by being lodged in cremation grounds and uninhabited wastelands as the presiding deity of wild tribes and robbers, or she is domesticated as the devotee's mother or child. In this latter idiom, she is depicted as a ferocious yet beautiful young woman with eyes that promise *kṛpā*, that is, grace and mercy, while in the former mode she is a fearsome, demonic figure with a disfigured, often skeletal body. It is in the image of Kālī that we find the characteristic predicament of patriarchal systems in dealing with female ownership of power while acknowledging the need for that power. Tracy Pintchman observes that, 'in the *Brahmanical* tradition, there is a strong tendency to portray *prakṛti, śakti,* and *māyā* on one level as positive and creative yet at the same time inherently ambiguous and potentially dangerous. Therefore they must be monitored and controlled so that they manifest their positive tendencies rather than their negative ones.'[55] Where the goddess is as threateningly powerful as Kālī, the way to assert control is either to keep the possessor of the power on the margins of the system or to keep her power in check by confining her within familial relationships.

Obviously, Kālī cannot be the source of any workable model for women within the order of power relationships of conventional society, which finds it more beneficial to press women into roles of service and submission derived from divine females. But that is precisely why in our own world, where questioning conventional order is viewed as a necessary task, particularly for women, Kālī has been drafted as the exemplar of a liberating energy implicit in women's nature. At the same time, the conformist impulse in social life is no less a part of our reality, which demands unambiguous guidelines, driving up the pressure, at least among present-day Hindus, to conserve the models of conduct for women derived from the religious foundations of their lives. It is a pleasing irony that those who battle conformity should equally borrow strength from a goddess, proving that these ancient constructions of the imagination still command modernity.

SECTION 2: SELECTED TEXTUAL PASSAGES WITH TRANSLATION*

Selected hymns and poems offered to Vedic goddesses

Uṣas

idam u tyat purutamaṃ purastāj
jyotis tamaso vayunāvadasthāt ǀ
nūnaṃ divo duhitaro vibhātīr
gātuṃ kṛṇavannuṣaso janāya ǀ ǀ

This familiar, most frequent light in the east, with clearness has stood (forth) from the darkness. Now may the Dawns, the daughters of the sky, shining afar, make a path for man.

(*ṚV*., iv.51: 1, Macdonell, ed. 1993 [1917], p. 93)

dyutadyāmānaṃ bṛhatīmṛtena
ṛtāvarīm aruṇapsuṃ vibhātīm ǀ
devīm uṣasaṃ svarāvahantīṃ
prati viprāso matibhir jarante ǀ ǀ

The priests greet with their prayers the divine Uṣas, the great one, who is shining, who is holy on account of *Ṛta*, the red-complexioned goddess who brings in the sun.

(*ṚV*., v.80: 1; Velankar, ed. 1972, p. 191)

Dyāvāpṛthivī

te hi dyāvāpṛthivī viśvaśaṃbhuvā
ṛtāvarī rajaso dhārayatkavī ǀ
sujanmanī dhiṣaṇe antarīyate
devo devī dharmaṇā sūryaḥ śuciḥ ǀ ǀ

These two, indeed, Heaven and Earth, are beneficial to all, observing order, supporting the sage of the air: between the two divine bowls that produce fair creations the divine bright Sūrya moves according to the fixed law.

(*ṚV*., i.160: 1; Macdonell, ed. 1993 [1917], p. 37)

* Unless otherwise indicated, translations are mine. Where translations by other sources are quoted, insertions in square brackets are mine.

. . . naḥ pavasva mātā bhūmiḥ putro ahaṃ pṛthivyāḥ I
parjanyaḥ pitā sa u naḥ pipartu I I

. . . [O mother earth!] Purify us. I am the son of earth. Earth is my mother. Cloud is my father. May it nourish us.
(*AtharvaVeda*, xii.1: 12; Devi Chand, ed. 1990 [1982], p. 532)

Aditi (with Viśvadevāḥ)

indraṃ mitraṃ varuṇam ūtaye
mārutaṃ śardho aditiṃ havāmahe I
rathaṃ na durgād vasavaḥ su dānavo
viśvasyaṃ no ahaṃ so niṣpipartana I I

We pray for protection to Indra, Mitra, Varuṇa with Maruts and Aditi. O the bestower of happiness, the Vasus! Protect us from all evil just as a chariot protects one on a rough road.
(*ṚV.*, i.106: 1; Āhitāgni, ed. 1991 [1904])

mātā devānām aditer anīkam . . .

The splendour of Aditi, the mother of the devas . . .
(*ṚV.*, i.113: 19; Āhitāgni, ed. 1991 [1904])

Vāc

ahaṃ rāṣṭrī saṅgamanī vasūnāṃ
cikituṣī prathamā yajñiyānām I
tāṃ mā devā vyadadhuḥ purutrā
bhūristhātrāṃ bhūryāveśayantīm I I

(*ṚV.*, x.125: 3)

I am the queen, bringer of wealth, skillful, foremost among the performers of the sacrifices. Gods divided me in many parts, manifested in many places and residing in many lives within myself.

Sarasvatī

codayditrī sunṛtānāṃ cetantī sumatīnāṃ yajñaṃ dadhe sarasvatī I I
(*ṚV.*, i.3: 11)

Sarasvatī, the inspirer of true and pleasing speech, the awakener of good conscience, upholds the sacrifice.

ayam u te sarasvati vasiṣṭho
dvārāvṛtasya subhage vyāvaḥ |
vardha śubhre stuvate rāsi
vājānyūyaṃ pāta svastibhiḥ sadā naḥ | |

This Vasiṣṭha has opened up the doors of the sacrifice for you, O, lovely Sarasvatī. Increase, O beautiful one and bestow gifts on the singer. Protect us with your favour always.
(*ṚV.*, vii.95: 6; Velankar, ed. 1972, p. 229)

Śṛī

hiraṇyavarṇāṃ hariṇīṃ suvarṇarajatasrajām |
candrāṃ hiraṇmayīṃ lakṣmīṃ jātavedo mā vaha | |
(*ṚV.*, Khilasūkta, v.87.1)

[I invoke you Agni] for Goddess Lakṣmī, who shines like gold, yellow in hue, wearing gold and silver garlands, like the moon, the embodiment of wealth. [Invoke for me] Lakṣmī, blessed by whom, I shall win.

Nirṛti

. . . *bahuprajā nirṛtim āviveśa* |
(*ṚV.*, i.164.32)

One who gives birth to many children enters Nirṛti (= the realm of suffering).
[Nirṛti is explained by philosophers as the realm of suffering while Yāska takes the term to denote the world.]
(*Niruktam*, 1955, pt. 1, pp. 234–5)

dūto nirṛtyā idam ājagāma . . .
(*ṚV.*, i.165.1)

A messenger has come here from the deity of death . . .
(*Niruktam*, 1955, pt. 1, p. 159)

[Most translators have translated Nirṛti as the world of suffering and deity of death.]

Rātri

atho yāni ca yasmā ha yāni cāntaḥ parīṇahi | *tāni te pari dadmasi* | |
rātri mātar uṣase naḥ pari dehi | *uṣā no ahṇe pari dadāt vahas tubhyaṃ vibhāvari* | |

O night, whatever we try to accumulate, and we lay hidden into the treasure-safe, we entrust all these to thee.
O bright, comfortable mother, night, entrust us to the dawn. Let the dawn entrust us to the day and the day again to thee.

(*AtharvaVeda*, xix.48: 1–2; Devi Chand, ed. 1990 [1982], p. 777)

Araṇyānī

ānjanagandhiṃ surabhiṃ bahvannām akṛṣīvalām |
prāhaṃ mṛgāṇāṃ mātaram araṇyānim aśaṃsiṣaṃ | |

I have well praised Araṇyāṇī; the mother of wild animals, emitting fragrance of unguents, sweet-scented, possessed of ample foods, though devoid of a farmer.

(*ṚV.*, x.146: 6; Velankar, ed. 1972, p. 308)

Post-Vedic goddesses

A Purāṇic tale about Sarasvatī in *Matsya Purāṇa*: Questioning Brahmā's action:

aho kaṣṭatarañcaitad aṅgajāgamanaṃ vibho |
kathaṃ na doṣam agamat karmeṇānena padmabhūḥ | | 1 | |
parasparañca sambandhaḥ sagotrāṇām abhūt katham |
vaivāhikas tat sutānāñchindhi me samśayaṃ vibho | | 2 | |
divyeyam ādisṛṣṭis tu rajoguṇasamudbhavā |
atīndriyendriyā tad vadatīndriyaśarīrikā | | 3 | |
divyatejomayī bhūpa divyajñānasamudbhavā |
na martyair amitaḥ śaktyā vaktuṃ vai māṃsacakṣubhiḥ | | 4 | |

(*Matsya Purāṇa*, iv.1–4)

[The king Vaivasvata Manu said;] O, [Lord], I am sad that the Omnipresent One approached his own daughter. Why, has he not committed a sin by acting this way? How [is this] relationship between *sagotras* [were allowed to] happen? O Lord, please remove my doubts [by explaining] why his offsprings were allowed to marry [between themselves]? [The Fish Avatāra replied] O King! Such doubts only arise in the case of mankind, for men have atomic bodies and beget children in a different way, while the primeval creation is celestial in which *rajoguṇa* predominates. The Devas are supersensory and they beget progeny in quite different ways. The celestial forms come into being in other ways and it is difficult for men having sensory bodies to understand this secret. Only supernatural intellect causes celestial creation; those alone understand its great secret who themselves are possessed of such an intellect.

Most commonly worshipped goddesses from the Purāṇic and the classical period

Lakṣmī

trailokyapūjite devi kamale viṣṇuvallabhe ।
yathā tvam acalā kṛṣṇe tathā bhava mayi sthitā ।।
īśvari kamale devi śaranam anaghe ।

(*Padmapurāṇa*, 4.11.36–7)

Devī, Kamalā, Viṣṇu's beloved, worshipped by the three worlds! As you remain constant to Kṛṣṇa, be constant to me. O Great Goddess Kamalā, Devī, faultless One, I take refuge with you.

Prayers for Lakṣmī in current use:

jaya padmapalāśākṣi jaya tvaṃ śripatipriye ।
jaya mātar mahālakṣmi saṃsārṇavatāriṇi ।।1।।
mahālakṣmi namastubhyaṃ namastubhyaṃ sureśvari ।
haripriye namastubhyaṃ namastubhyaṃ dayānidhe ।।2।।

(Agastikṛtaṃ Lakṣmistrotram, *Stavakavacamālā*, Gupta and Bhrigu, coll. and ed. n.d., p. 151)

Glory to thee! O the lotus-eyed one! O Śṛī, beloved of lord, glory to thee!
Glory to mother Mahālakṣmi, deliverer from the ocean of this world!
I bow to thee, Mahālakṣmi again and again, foremost among gods,
I bow to thee, beloved of Hari, again and again, O Jewel of Compassion!

Om, trailokyapūjite devi kamale viṣṇuvallabhe ।
yathā tvaṃ susthirā kṛṣṇe tathā bhava mayi sthirā ।
īsvarī kamalā lakṣmī acalā bhūtir haripriyā ।
padmā padmālayā sampad ramā śrī padmadhāriṇī । ।
dvādaśaitāni nāmāni lakṣmīṃ sampūjya yaḥ paṭhet ।
sthirā lakṣmī bhavet tasya putradāradibhiḥ saha । ।

Om! Devī, Kamalā, Viṣṇu's beloved, worshipped by the three worlds! As you remain constant to Kṛṣṇa, be constant to me. Īśvarī, Kamalā, Lakṣmī, Constancy, Prosperity, Beloved of Hari, Padmā, Abode of Lotus, Wealth, Beauty, Splendour, Holder of Lotus – one who recites these twelve names after worshipping Lakṣmī, Lakṣmī remains constant to him with his wife and sons.

(A prayer used for worshipping Mahālakṣmī every Thursday)

Sarasvatī

vāgdaivatyaiś ca carubhir yajeraṃste sarasvatīm ।
anṛtasyainasastasya kurvāṇā niṣkṛtiṃ parām । ।

(*Manusmṛti*, 8.105)

Those who desire absolute freedom from the guilt of falsehood should sacrifice to Sarasvatī with consecrated bowls of porridge dedicated to the goddess of speech.

sarasvatīṃ śuklavarṇāṃ sasmitāṃ sumanoharām ।
koṭicandraprabhāmuṣṭapuṣṭaśrīyuktavigrahāṃ । ।
. . .
supūjitāṃ suragaṇair brahmāviṣṇuśivādibhiḥ ।
vande bhaktyā vanditāṃ tāṃ munīndramanumānavaiḥ । ।

(*Brahmavaivartapurāṇa: prakṛtikhanda*, 15.21, 23)

The fair-complexioned Sarasvatī who appears with a pleasant smile, who surpasses even the effulgence of a million moons, who is adorned with beauty is worshipped by gods such as Brahmā, Viṣṇu and Śiva. Devotees, such as Manu, greatest among the sages, and ordinary human beings, pay obeisance to her.

A prayer to Sarasvatī in current use:

śvetapadmāsanā devī śvetapuṣpopśobhitā ।
śvetāmbaradharā devī śvetagandhānulepanā । ।

śvetākṣasūtrahastā ca śvetacandanacarcitā ।
śvetavīṇādharā śubhrā śvetālaṅkārabhūṣitā । ।
vanditā siddhagandharvair arcitā suradānavaiḥ ।
pūjitā munibhiḥ sarvai ṛṣibhiḥ stūyate sadā । ।
stotreṇānena tāṃ devīm jagaddhātrīṃ sarasvatīm ।
ye smaranti trisandhyāyāṃ sarvāṃ vidyāṃ labhanti te । ।

(From *Stavakavacamālā*, Gupta and Bhrigu, coll. and ed., n.d., p. 172)

The goddess, seated on a white lotus, adorned with white flowers, wearing a white dress, perfumed by white scent, holding a rosary in her hand, decorated with sandalwood paste is always worshipped by *siddhas* and *gandharvas*, gods and demons, sages and saints. Those who remember Goddess Sarasvatī, the protector of the world, with this prayer three times [*sandhyās*] a day, will gain all knowledge.

Durgā

Prayers to Durgā in current use:

devī prapannārtihare prasīda
prasīda mātarjagato'khilasya ।
prasīda viśveśvari pāhi viśvaṃ
tvamīśvarī devi carcarasya । ।

(*Durgāsaptaśatī*, 11.3, Sharma, ed. 2000, pp. 149–150; from *Devīmāhātmyam* in *Mārkaṇḍeya Purāṇa*)

O Goddess, the remover of afflictions of the suppliants, be pleased. O the mother of the whole world, be pleased. O the queen of the universe, be pleased; protect the universe. O Goddess, you are the mistress of the movables and immovables.

yā devī sarvabhūteṣu śaktirūpeṇa samsthitā ।
namastasyai namastasyai namastyai namo namaḥ । ।
. . .
yā devī sarvabhūteṣu mātṛrūpeṇa samsthitā ।
namastasyai namastasyai namastyai namo namaḥ । ।

(*Durgāsaptaśatī*, 5.32–4, 5.71–3, Sharma, ed. 2000, p. 76, p. 80; from *Devīmāhātmyam* in *Mārkaṇḍeya Purāṇa*)

I bow to thee ! I bow to thee ! I bow to thee ! O, Goddess, who resides in every living being as power and energy, I bow to thee!

. . .

I bow to thee ! I bow to thee ! I bow to thee ! O, Goddess, who resides in every living being as mother, I bow to thee!

Daśamahāvidyās

A chant in common use:

kālī tārā mahāvidyā ṣoḍaśī bhuvaneśvarī |
bhairavī chinnamastā ca vidyā dhūmāvatī tathā | |
bagalā siddhividyā ca mātaṅgī kamalātmikā |
etā daśa mahāvidyā siddhavidyā prakīrtitāḥ | |

Kālī, Tārā, Ṣoḍaśī, Bhuvaneśvarī, Bhairvī, Chinnamastā, Dhūmāvatī, Bagalā, Mātaṅgī, Kamalā are known as the ten Mahāvidyās.

Kālī

kālikāyai namastubhyam iti yo bhāṣate svayam |
tasya haste sthitā muktis trivargas tu vaśānugaḥ | |
(*Kālikāpurāṇam*, Tarkaratna and Nyayatirtha, ed. 1977, 90.28)

One who prays [everyday] saying, I bow to thee Kālikā, within his hands reside liberation and under [his] control all three *vargas* [*dharma, artha, kāma*].

kalanāt sarvabhūtānāṃ mahākālaḥ prakīrtitaḥ |
mahākālasya kalanāt tvam ādyā kālikā parā | |
(*Mahānirvāṇatantra*, Misra ed. 1985, 4.31)

Since Kāla (time) devours everything, it is named Mahākāla. By devouring Mahākāla You have become the Foremost, Kālikā and the Ultimate.

A prayer currently in use for worshipping Kālī:

Om! Kāli Kāli Mahākāli Kālike pāpahāriṇi |
dharmārthamokṣade Devi Nārāyaṇi namo'stute | |
(*Kālī Pūjā*, Saraswati, ed. 1998, p. 246)

Om! [Goddess] Kālī ! Great Kālī ! Remover of sins! I bow to thee, O Goddess! Who shows [lit: gives] [the path of] righteousness, material success and [ultimate] liberation.

A verse from Rāmprasād Sen:

e sab kṣepā māyer khelā,
yār māyāy tribhuvan bibholā | |

(Bhattacharya 1975, *padāvalī* 65)

All this is crazy Mother's play,
Whose *māyā* leaves the three worlds deluded.

Another:

e sakal to tor-i māyā, bājikarer bājīr mato |
. . .
dine dine din gelo mā, supath khuṃje pelām nāto |
ghor niśā ye āsche tārā, apathe ār ghuri kato | |

(Bhattacharya 1975, *padāvalī*, 306)

All this is but your *māyā,* like a magician's trick
. . .
O Mother, day after day goes by,
I still have not found the right way,
O Tara, with dark nights approaching,
How much longer shall I roam about the wrong way.

Sītā

pātālete prabeśiyā tileka nā thāki |
vaikuṇṭhe svamūrti dhari gelen jānakī | |
vaikkuṇṭhe gelen lakṣmī hṛṣṭa devagaṇa |
ayodhyā nagare hethā uṭhila krandana | |

(*Kṛttibāsī Rāmāyaṇa*, H. Mukhopadhyaya, ed., 1989, 7, p. 527)

After entering *pātāla* [the nether world] Jānakī did not stay there for a moment and went straight to *vaikuṇṭha* in her own form. Gods were pleased when Lakṣmī went to *vaikuṇṭha* [but] here in the city of Ayodhyā wailing arose.

[Sītā is identified with Lakṣmī in Kṛttibāsa's Bengali *Rāmāyaṇa*.]

udbhavasthitisaṃhārakāriṇīṃ kleśahāriṇīm |
sarvaśreyaskarīṃ sītāṃ nato'haṃ rāmavallabhām | |

I bow before Sītā, the beloved of Rāma, the cause of creation, preservation and dissolution, the destroyer of sorrow and the source of all blessings.

(Tulasīdās. *Shriramacaritamanasa*, R. C Prasad, ed. and tr., 1999, *Bālakāṇḍa, maṅgalācaraṇa*, verse 5, p. 1)

Rādhā

vāgdevatācaritacitritacittasadmā
padmāvatīcaraṇacāraṇacakravartī |
śrīvāsudevaratikelikathāsametam
etaṃ karoti jayadevakaviḥ prabandham | |

Jayadeva, wandering king of bards
Who sings at Padmāvatī's lotus feet,
Was obsessed in his heart
By rhythms of the goddess of speech,
And he made this lyrical poem
From tales of the passionate play
When Kṛṣṇa loved Śrī.

(Jayadeva, *Gītagovinda*, Miller, ed. and tr. 1977, 1.2, p. 69, p.129)

[Jayadeva identifies Rādhā as Śrī.]

rūpa-rāsi, sukha rāsi rādhike, sīla mahā guna rāsi |
kṛṣṇa-carana te pāvahi syāmā, je tuva carana upāsī | |

(Sūrdās, *Sūrsāgar*, NPS ed. 1964, 10.1055.1673, verse 12, p. 624)

Rādhikā, jewel of joy and of beauty,
A treasure, a gem of the finest quality,
Those who bring to your lotus feet love
Through love attain also Kṛṣṇa's.

(Hawley 1986, p. 51)

Notes

1 Pintchman 1994, Introduction, p. 18.
2 For a general view of the periodization, see Embree 1988 [1958].
3 Macdonell 1993 [1917], p. 92.
4 Gupta in Bose 2000, p. 103.
5 *Vājasaneyīa Samhitā* of *Śuklayajurveda*, xix.80–95.
6 *Śatatapatha Brāhmaṇa* 14.2.1.12; *Aitareya Brāhmaṇa* 6.7.
7 Bhattacharji 1970, p. 160
8 *Śatatapatha Brāhmaṇa* 2.2.1.19; *Aitareya Brāhmaṇa* 1.8.
9 *Śatatapatha Brāhmaṇa* 12.5.5.12
10 Kinsley 1986, p. 13.
11 Many Hindu women, irrespective of caste, worship her daily, weekly, monthly and annually.
12 Bhattacharji 1970, p. 162.
13 Ibid. pp. 162–3.
14 Ibid. p. 296.
15 Tripathi in Sircar 1970, pp. 158–62.
16 Parallels to Śrī (Dewi Siri) can also be found in Indo-China and Indonesia; see Bhattacharji 1970, pp. 161–2.
17 Behera in Sircar 1970, pp. 91–105.
18 Bhattacharji 1970, p. 296.
19 Kinsley 1986, p. 16.
20 For detailed descriptions and discussion of goddesses see Bhattacharji 1970, and Kinsley 1986.
21 Bhattacharji 1970, pp. 79, 146.
22 Ibid. p. 89.
23 In *Manusmṛti* 2.17 and 11.78, Sarasvatī appears as a river and the land that it irrigates is referred to as the land of the Vedas where one purifies oneself.
24 Chatterjee in Sircar 1970, pp. 148–52.
25 *Brahmavaivarta Purāṇa, Prakṛti Khaṇḍa* 5.21–7. The same section, however, classifies women into two categories, chaste and unchaste (16.61–72).
26 See Flood 1996, pp. 174–97, and Gupta 1972, pp. 27–34 for the philosophical interpretation of this relationship between *puruṣa* and *prakṛti*.
27 Bhattacharji 1970, p. 14.
28 Ibid. p. 160.
29 Ibid. p. 123.
30 *Rām* i.35.16. It is likely that Kālidāsa found the seed of his *Kumārsambhava* in the verse that follows: *Rām* i.37.31.
31 *HV*. iii.88.
32 Bhattacharji 1970, p. 177; *Mbh*, xiii.14.298–313.
33 See O'Flaherty in Hawley and Wulff 1982 for a fuller discussion of myths of *Pārvatī;* also, O'Flaherty 1975, pp. 238–69.
34 *Devīmāhātmya* is part of *Mārkaṇḍeya Purāṇa* written around the 6th century C.E.
35 *yā devī sarvabhūteṣu viṣṇumāyeti śabditā* |
namastasyai namastasyai namastasyai namo namah | |
(*Durgāsaptaśatī*, 5.14, p. 89)
36 Bhattacharji 1970, pp. 167–8

37 See Bhattacharji 1970, pp. 161–76 for a comprehensive and comparative discussion of Durgā. Bhattacharji compares her with goddesses from the ancient civilizations of the Middle East as well as from various sources within India.
38 Kinsley 1975, p. 144.
39 Flood 1996, p. 187.
40 Ibid. pp. 183–4.
41 A detailed discussion of Sītā as a role model for Indian women appears in Pauwels 2008, pp. 8–12. Madhu Kishwar's interviews with women in modern India question Sītā's submissiveness (*Manushi*, 1997, no. 98, pp. 21–34).
42 Monier-Williams 1964 [1899], p. 1218.
43 *Sītā Lakṣmī* . . . *VR*. vi.117.27.
44 Except in some little known retellings of the epic from a *śākta* angle, such as the eighteenth-century Bengali language *Jagadrāmī-Rāmprasādī Rāmāyaṇa*.
45 Thomas Coburn *Mānushī*, no. 90 (September–October, 1995).
46 In February 2008 there was serious controversy at Delhi University over teaching an essay by A. K. Ramanujan, 'Three Hundred *Ramayananas*', which discusses regional versions of the *Rāmāyaṇa*, in some of which Sîtā has a prominent role with a voice of her own. The *Akhil Bhartiya Vidyarthi Parishad* (*ABVP*), a group of orthodox Hindus, objected to that finding. *Hindustan Times*, a major Indian newspaper reported: 'The *ABVP* is saying that *Tulsi Ramayana* and *Valmiki Ramayana* are the only two versions of the *Ramayana* that are valid' (26 February 2008). The *Vālmikī Rāmāyaṇa* is in Sanskrit and very few people have access to it. Therefore, it is Tulasī's version which, according to *ABVP*, should shape the popular mind.
47 *VR*. vi.119.5.
48 An example of this ideological orientation appears in Jacqueline Suthrenhirst's *Sītā's Story*, written for Indian girl children in the UK.
49 Kinsley 1986, pp. 85–92. For a fuller understanding of Rādhā's love for Kṛṣṇa, see Barbara Stoler Miller, *Love Song of the Dark Lord* (New York: Columbia University Press, 1977).
50 See Kinsley 1986, pp. 82–3; Miller 1977, pp. 29–30.
51 For a more modern interpretation of Sītā and Rādhā based on recent movies as well as scriptures, see Pauwels 2008.
52 Kinsley 1986, pp. 197–204.
53 Flood 1996, p. 197.
54 Gupta in Bose 2000, p. 87.
55 Pintchman 1994, p. 18.

3 Shaping women's lives

SECTION 1: THE ROLE OF ANCIENT HINDU TEXTS*

> Judgements on the nature of women, their roles in society, and injunctions on dealing with women form important parts of Brahminical texts of sacred law going back to early India. These constitute a continuing discourse on gender that includes debate and controversy but nevertheless establishes the subordination of women on the social plane, which, this chapter argues, is facilitated by the idealization of women as icons of virtue and the deification of the female.

When we are speaking of a social world that is close to two millennia old, it is hard to know exactly what the conditions of people's lives were in the beginning, or, for that matter, through much of its evolution. We have to rely for our knowledge on the one hand on textual material of the widest variety, comprising religious, literary and sociological treatises, and on the other hand on surviving social customs and practices. In the present study, my attempt to understand how women have been thought of in early Hindu society will be based on evidence from textual sources, beginning with Vedic texts. As we confront this vast repository of thought, it is difficult not to be struck by surprise that so much energy was spent on thinking about women. Why was this necessary? Were women considered such alien creatures

* Unless otherwise indicated, translations are mine.

that theories had to be formulated about their nature and dispensations framed to manage every step they took? It is tempting to answer 'Yes', but such certainty may be premature, for an alternative explanation could lie in the cultural tradition of India to subject all phenomena and all ideas to the minutest and ceaseless scholarly scrutiny to the point of overkill. Whatever the true reason for the proliferation of pronouncements on women, it provides the present-day scholar with a rich trove of textual material on questions of gender. As a matter both of intellectual curiosity and social policy, then, the textual discourse of women in the formative ages of Hindu culture demands scrutiny. Of this extensive material I can present here only samples to create a sense, a reliable sense, I hope, of what the early Hindus thought about women, taking their views thematically, for instance, in terms of attitudes to girl children, mothers, wives, women's education, inheritance, personal wealth and duties and, in particular, the essential nature of women.

In weighing the evidence of the texts we must proceed with caution because they do not always speak with one voice. Not unexpectedly for a discourse that addresses as complex a question as how humans *ought to* live with one another, the vast literature of early India that occupies itself with ethical models of social living contains frequent contradictions and magisterial fiats that may well seem based more on prejudice than on reason. In particular, controversies swirl around views on the most pre-eminent issue of all, the desirability of the birth of a girl child. Is it to be welcomed or lamented? I shall begin with this primary question, reviewing recorded views from the earliest available textual sources, drawing upon primary texts rather than glosses or annotative commentaries, and shall follow up by turning to the conditions of female life in society, such as, their right to education and their access to it, their duties, ritual rights, property rights and responsibilities as women, and in general their position in society. I shall also pay particular attention to two vital issues, first, *strīdhana* or women's personal wealth and their rights to wealth (*svatva* and *svāmitva*), and second, *punarvivāha* or the remarriage of a woman. Since these are prescriptive judgements, they imply the need for implementation, which brings us to the realm of social policy and practice, that is, the actual conditions of women's life. In terms of academic discipline, those conditions constitute the domain of the social historian and the anthropologist, who have indeed been exploring the field for a long time as will be evident from the bibliography for this chapter.[1] What I offer here is a look at the platform on which the enabling debate behind social practice took place. This is not a comprehensive history of women's situation in the Hindu world, but I hope this discussion will serve to reveal the lines along which the ideas of womanhood and women's lives have been constructed in Hindu society.

To complement the testimony of the sacred texts of Hindu society and their texts of law and conduct, which are of course normative statements, with statements of emotional and imaginative response, I shall present material from the two major epics of India and some dramas. It would be obviously impractical to try to bring the entire body of Sanskrit literature within the scope of this book. Although gender is not in itself made into an issue in Sanskrit literature, it does abound in responses to women, adverse as well as sympathetic. Of particular interest will be literary statements on daughters because they illuminate the contentious and, as I have remarked above, primary issue of what amounts to be the very right of women to life. Beyond the prescriptions of the law books and sacred texts, there exist descriptions and evaluations of basic, everyday relationships in the literary representation of women. Even though the lives depicted and the sentiments laid bare in literature relate mainly to women of privileged and educated families, we can still derive from literature a keen sense of their lives within family relationships played out within the web of everyday personal exchanges.

To place the discourse of gender on the scale of history, we shall begin our search for evidence in the Vedic texts. Beginning in the Vedic era as occasional or, sometimes, incidental comments on women, the tradition of commentary grew into a targeted discourse by the time of the *dharmaśāstras*, which laid down rules comprehensively and exactly to define women's place in the world. It is a discourse that deals exclusively with women's place in family life, expectations from them, and their nature. Its most striking features are its immense extent and its unrelenting contradictoriness. That women are so constantly in view, and that opinions about their nature and regulations encompassing their lives occur everywhere, suggests that the question of women remained an unresolved one throughout the literature we have at hand. This no doubt explains the variety, including the contradictions, within the discourse, in which opinions and expositions take opposite positions. While this variance makes it difficult for us to judge precisely to what extent scholarly views reflected or determined women's lives in the actual world of social relations, it does attest to the vigour of the intellectual tradition and, despite the authoritarianism of opinion, its readiness to consider alternative viewpoints.

An intriguing element in the discourse of women is that in some texts they appear not just as social beings but almost as a separate species, with roles and treatment assigned to them on the basis of an essentialist view of women's nature. Certain characteristics, these texts state, are essential to women without reference to the temporal or social context they occupy. Thus, the discourse on women varies from prescription and description to assertion. A great many of the texts prescribe what women should do in the home and how they should be regarded and treated. Others, some by highly influential authors, describe a notional woman on the basis of what they assert is the essential nature of womankind, often in the most intemperate tone. This in itself is worth a separate discussion as a conundrum, particularly as it is characteristic of the great lawgiver Manu, who is credited with issuing strict injunctions to revere women as well as with a perverse attribution to women of a sexual appetite bestial in its lack of self-restraint.[2] We must also bear in mind that Manu is only one, though perhaps the best known and most reviled, of the ancient authorities on law, known as the *smṛtikāras* who expatiated on women and set down injunctions for them, and that the rules laid down by them or derived from their views were put into actual practice followed in ancient and medieval Hindu society. Like Manu's remarks, those by other *smṛtikāras* are often contradictory, rendering the entire discourse gravely confusing when we try to compile a tidy, homogenous package and label it the Hindu View of Women. That view, one must acknowledge, is not homogenous. Indeed, it is the heterogeneity of the views that ought to be marked as proof of the vigour of the discursive tradition in India. That is why we must begin at the beginning, with Vedic literature and see how the discourse began.

Comments and views on women in Vedic literature range widely. Not only do the texts recommend prayers for the birth of sons and for avoiding the birth of daughters (*Kṛṣṇayajurveda*, 1.1.64), noting in passing that the birth of a daughter spells misfortune for her father, they also suggest how wives should be treated and how wives should conduct themselves. Injunctions concerning women are uniformly framed within women's relationships with men, as daughters, wives and mothers, who are viewed as attachments to men and never as independent persons on their own. Women's sphere is exclusively the home and their action confined to the family. While we know that some women were revered because of their intellectual ability, such as the *brahmavādinīs* (learned women) of the Vedic era and the female sages of later times, women are never considered in the framework of public life, such as in political roles. Although much is made of the reverence due to mothers (but mostly to mothers who could produce sons), we see that as time goes by, the emphasis in the literature of social regulations shifts decisively to women's role as wives, with an ever-increasing demand for unquestioning servitude to husbands.[3]

The discourse on women generally records a preference for sons over daughters, the birth of a girl child being usually considered a misfortune. One of our earliest sources, the *ṚgVeda* records prayers in *sūkta* 8.4, 6. (*putraṃ prāvargaṃ kṛṇute subīrye dāśnoti nama uktibhiḥ*), for the birth of sons and declares the birth of a daughter to be inauspicious. The *Aitareya Brāhmaṇa* extends this partiality by declaring that a daughter is a form of misery (*kṛpaṇam*), that a son is a light in the highest heaven (3.33.1), and that a sonless person cannot attain heaven (3.7.13).[4] Sometimes the anxiety over the possibility of giving birth to a daughter rises so high that nothing short of occult prophylactics will do to guard against it. The *Kṛṣṇayajurveda*, for example, recommends abstaining from the ritual arrangement of *kuśa* grass to avoid the birth of a girl child saying that, 'the birth of a daughter spells misfortune for a father. Abstain from ritual arrangements to avoid the birth of a girl child' (1.1.64).[5] This apprehension over daughters becomes savage in the *Atharvaveda*, which is not content with stating that a daughter is not seen as auspicious but goes on to recommend that a girl child should be put away (6.11.3). *Taittirīya Saṃhitā* concurs with this judgement recommending that daughters are to be subjected to *'parāsyanti'*, which literally means 'alienated', that is, abandoned in order to bring about death (6.5.10). The barbarity of this solution was clearly too much to stomach for everybody, for in a later, though not necessarily more sympathetic age, Sāyanācārya attempted to explain it away by interpreting the term *'parāsyanti'* as the act of transferring a daughter to another family by marriage, which is obviously a beneficial act (*varakule parityajanti*). He also says that since a daughter will be inevitably married off, bringing about the pain of separation to her parents, she should be especially cared for as long as she is in her parents' home. Manu says that one's daughter is the supreme subject of pity, *'duhitā kṛpaṇam param'* (*Manusmṛti*, 4.185).

Countervailing voices such as Sāyanācārya's are few. Daughters are seldom viewed with joy, rare examples being the *Bṛhadāraṇyaka Upaniṣad* (6.4.9) and the *Nirukta* (2.4), both of which attribute the begetting of a daughter not just to the body but to the heart, which therefore requires that she be lovingly cared for. Another text that approves of daughters is the *Matsyapurāṇa*, which reminds us that 'no progeny can be born without a woman', that 'in the *śāstras* at many places it has been said that a girl is equal to ten sons' (2.154.157), and that 'the birth of a daughter brings high merit' (2.154.414). Much later we see the same love for a daughter in the *Abhijnānaśakuntalam*, in which a particularly tender verse in Act 4, verse 6 expresses a father's sadness at his daughter's departure for her husband's home. A still later work, the *Harṣacarita*, expresses the same sadness at losing a daughter when in Act 4 Rājyaśrī's mother speaks of her impending marriage.

But the common attitude is one of bemoaning the birth of daughters and expressing a longing for sons. The *Rāmāyaṇa* and the *Mahābhārata*, perhaps the most accessible and influential texts for the majority of Hindus, echo these sentiments, both agreeing that those who desire honour do not wish to be the father of a daughter (*Rāmāyaṇa*: *Uttarakāṇḍa*, 9.10, *Mahābhārata*: *Udyogaparva*, 97.16). The *Mahābhārata* goes a step farther by remarking that to have a daughter born to them is a misery for the parents (*Ādiparva*, 159.11). Similarly, the *Pañcatantra* says that the birth of a daughter spells anxiety for a father.

This aversion to daughters is hard to understand when considered against the standard view of early Hindu thinkers that girls should receive education, and the historical reality of women celebrated for their intellectual and spiritual attainments. For example, the supposed anxiety of parents at the prospect of a daughter being born does not fit in with the *Bṛhadāraṇyaka Upaniṣad's* advice to parents to perform a *yajña* to ensure the birth of a daughter who will be a '*paṇḍitā*', i.e., a savant (6.4.17). But again as an illustration of the contradictions within the gender discourse, let me refer to Śankara, who offers the forced reinterpretation of the term '*paṇḍitā*' as one well-versed in household duties, which reflects his decidedly conservative outlook. But so many early writers advocate education for girls, initiation in the sacred thread rituals, and the right and responsibility to participate in *yajñas*, that such provisions cannot be regarded as anything but commonly accepted conditions of women's upbringing. Hārita [eighth century C.E.] mentions *upanayana* for women, saying that they should be initiated by age 8 and educated (*Smṛticandrikā* p. 24), and goes further still to say that women can be either *sadyavadhūs* (housewives) or *brahmavādinīs*, a term which he invents to denote learned women. Yama similarly advocates *upanayana* for women and accords them the right to recite the *sāvitrī mantra*, although he restricts their education to tutelage under their fathers, brothers or uncles. The *Gobhila Gṛhyasūtra* (2.1.19) refers to '*yajnopavītinī*' women, the feminine ending of the term clearly indicating that women were allowed to wear the sacred threads.[6]

The provision, or perhaps the requirement, of education for women in the early period becomes more significant in the higher reaches of intellectual activity, where we encounter the many learned women of Vedic times, including composers of Vedic hymns and *brahmavādinīs* who were celebrated intellectuals, mentioned, for instance, in *Bṛhaddevata*. Among them were Ghoṣā, Godhā, Viśvavārā (also in *ṚV*. 5.28), Apālā (also in *ṚV*. 8.91), Upaniṣat, Niṣat, Brahmajāyā Juhu, Agastyasvasā, Aditi, Indrāṇī, Indramātā, Saramā, Romaśā, Urvaśī, Lopāmudrā, Nadī, Yamī, Nārī, Śaśvatī, Śrī, Lākṣā, Sārparājñī, Vāk, Śraddhā, Medhā, Dakṣiṇā, Rātrī, Sūryā and Sāvitrī (*Bṛhaddevatā*, 2.82–4). Evidently, male savants did not deem women unworthy of engaging in scholarly discussion, as we learn from the encounter between Maitreyī and Yājñavalkya (*Bṛ Upa*. 2.4.1–4) and the oft-cited Gārgī-Yājñavalkya debate (*Bṛ Upa*. 3.6). When asked by her husband Yājñavalkya, Maitreyī refuses material wealth and wants to join him in his quest for immortality because, she asks, 'Of what use would wealth be to me if it does not bring immortality?'. In Gargī's legend, at the end of a lengthy debate she finally presses Yājñavalkya with a series of questions. She asks, 'On what then are woven the worlds of Prajāpati?'. Yājñavalkya answers, 'On the worlds of Brahman, O Gārgī.' After several other philosophical queries comes her final question, 'On what then are woven the worlds of Brahman?'. The answer is, 'Do not ask an improper question, so that your head may not fall off.' Gārgī then falls silent. This of course seems to be a piece of patriarchal authoritarianism; or it may simply indicate a senior scholar rebuking an overreaching junior. Or, more intriguingly, it may reflect the inadvisability of probing matters beyond mortal comprehension to the metaphoric point of losing one's head. But the real point of the legend is that quite aside from whatever gender implications the legend may or may not have, it places Gārgī unambiguously within collegial reach of the great sages of her time. That women such as Gārgī were recognized as teachers as well, is clear from a reference in the *Kāśikā* commentary on Pāṇini to women *ācāryās* and *upādhyāyās*, who were distinct from *ācāryanīs* and *upādhyāyānis*, that is, wives of teachers. Patañjali mentions a number of female grammarians who were viewed as *āpiśalā*, and *mīmāmsakā* women as *kāśakṛtsnas*, thus including women as members of prestigious schools of thought in his time. Various *śrauta* and *gṛhyasūtras* recommend that wives should utter *mantras* at *yajñas*, and Gobhila (1.3.15) stresses that if the wife wishes to, she may perform *yajñas* both in the morning and in the evening, which implies that Gobhila is taking for granted a high educational level for such wives, and thus, the need for educating women. However, Gobhila also instructs that at a daughter's *cūḍākaraṇa* (as well as other *saṃskāras*), unlike that of a son's, no *mantras* should be uttered, except at the time of fire sacrifice (2.9.21–4). *Taittirīya*

Saṃhitā (6.1.4–6) and *Śatapatha Brāhmaṇa* (3.2.4.3–6) refer to dance and music learned and performed by women, including performances in public. In the *Rāmāyaṇa, yajñas* are performed by Kausalyā (*Rāmāyaṇa, Ayodhyākāṇḍa,* 20.14). Śabarī is well-known as a sage, with an *āśrama* of her own where she practised her religious life (*Rāmāyaṇa, Araṇyakāṇḍa,* 74.4; 74.7–8). In the *Mahābhārata,* both Sābitrī and Ambā perform *yajñas*, and Kuntī obtains esoteric *mantras.* Satyavatī, the matriarch of the Kuru dynasty, instructs the male members of the family on *dharmic* actions, and everyone concurs: *satyavatī mate sthitaḥ* (*Ādiparva,* 95.5; 96.1; 96.59). We may also bear in mind that knowledge and the arts are taken to be the domain of the goddess Sarasvatī.

The widespread reverence for learned women and the willingness on the part of many thinkers to accord women the right to education does not, however, mitigate the more general disdain for women. That the denigration of women was founded on an understanding of women not only as lesser beings to men but also as moral defectives are amply evidenced in texts in every age, although why they are so viewed remains a mystery. Against all evidence of women's intellectual accomplishments, the *ṚgVeda* dismisses female intelligence, stating that 'The mind of women brooks no discipline', and that 'her intellect has little weight' (8.33.17). No wonder then that the *ṚgVeda* should deny daughters a share in patrimony (3.3.1), while the *Taittirīya Saṃhitā* (6.5.8.2), cited in the *Baudhāyana Dharmasūtra* (2.3.46), denies women legal rights altogether. The *Rāmāyaṇa* refers to the essential nature of women as fickle, untrustworthy and cruel in more than one place (*Rāmāyaṇa, Araṇyakāṇḍa,* 13.6; 45.30).

The issue of inheritance again illustrates the contradiction in opinion that I have mentioned as typical of the Hindu discourse on women. If the *ṚgVeda* and other authorities deny women inheritance and other legal rights, there are many who endorse such rights. The *Nirukta* (3.4–5) provides for daughters to inherit their father's property on being appointed by the father for the purpose, and Gautama similarly counsels men who have no sons to allow their daughters to inherit their property (28.18) and advises that the wife's property should go to her daughters if they are unmarried or indigent (28.24). Forcefully rationalizing the rights of daughters to property, Bṛhaspati argues that since a daughter is born from the same human body as a son, there is no reason why a father's wealth should be taken by another person (25.56).

The refusal of many authorities to allow women inheritance rights is not surprising if we place it against the judgement they pass on women's character as a general truth, centring both on women's mental incapacity and their moral frailty. Not only does the *Ṛg Veda* dismiss women as thinking beings, as we have already seen, but it also cautions men against women's moral constitution when it declares that, 'with women there can be no friendship', presumably because in its view, 'the hearts of hyenas are the hearts of women' (10.95.15). The image is worth noting, for it attributes to women not just untrustworthiness but cruelty and rapacity. The *Pañcatantra* says that the essential nature of a woman is falsehood, ignorance and deception (*Mitrabheda*, 207). It is not pleasant to catalogue these dismal views but we must not ignore the most widely known authority on Hindu conduct, the legendary Manu, to whose pronouncements on women much of the restrictions and degradation of women's life in modern times have been traced. But again, these injunctions are marked by the contradiction that I have mentioned as characteristic of the discourse on women.

To put it briefly, Manu at once adulates and condemns women. Let me cite some of his opinions in praise of women:

> 3.55: Those fathers, brothers, husbands and brothers-in-law who desire much prosperity should esteem [these] women and adorn them.
> 3.56: Where women are respected, the deities rejoice, but where they are not respected, all rituals become fruitless.

It is therefore with incredulity that one goes on to other chapters of the *Manusmṛti* in which we are informed that:

> 2.213: To corrupt men in the world is women's essential nature. Therefore, wise men do not heedlessly seek pleasure among wanton women.
> 9.2: Men should keep women in thrall through the day and night. Attached to material things, [women] must be kept in control [by other women].
> 9.3: In childhood, her father shields her; in youth, her husband shields her; in her old age her son shields her: a woman never earns independence.
> 9.10: A woman cannot be kept in check by any man by force alone. However, by using the following ways it is possible to control them:
> 9.11: She should be engaged in the conserving and disposing of wealth, in purifying [rituals], in doing her duties, in cooking meals and in caring for household goods.

9.12: Women cannot be guarded [even when] confined inside a house by trustworthy men. Those women who watch over themselves are well protected.
9.13: Drinking, keeping bad company, absence from spouses, roaming about, sleeping and living in someone else's home, are the six [vices] that corrupt women.
9.14: They do not care about the looks, nor do they care about the age [of a man]. Whether handsome or ugly, 'a man' she enjoys.
9.15: They are like harlots, fickle-minded and by nature uncaring. Even when they are well guarded by their husbands, they are unfaithful.
9.16: Realizing that [women] are by nature like this as created by the Lord of Creatures, a man must take special effort to watch over [them].
9.17: The bed, the seat, ornaments, sensual desire, anger, vulgarity, exploitation, bad behaviour are ascribed to women's nature by Manu.
9.18: There are no rituals with sacred verses for women according to the law established. Women, who have no virility and power from sacred verses, are but falsehood. This is well established.[7]

Can this be the same sage who asserts that 'where women are respected, the deities rejoice' (*Manu*, 3.56)? Putting aside the vileness of the later comments, let us consider the themes underlying them. One insistent idea is that women need to be both protected and guarded, because they are weak in body and mind and unfit for independence. Equally important is the thesis that in addition to weakness, women are characterized by greed and duplicity, such that they can be kept under control by being bribed with wealth, while their innate deceitfulness means that they are best protected from their own moral infirmity by other women, since women best understand one another's wiles. Yet another flaw inherent in womanhood is fickleness, understood not only as a mental frailty but also, and more seriously, as a moral laxity, namely, an appetite for sexual incontinence that makes women disgustingly bestial in its compulsive pursuit. Threaded through these observations is a fear of women who have the power and evidently the will to corrupt men (2.213), who must therefore watch their step with women. At the centre of this abhorrence of women lies an axiomatic understanding of women's inherent nature, 'as created by the Lord of Creatures' (9.16). Such is the essence of womanhood presumed in Manu's attribution of women's affinity with the bed and the seat, that is, with indolence, jewellery, lust and anger, crookedness, malice and general 'bad behaviour' (9.17). Women, he says, are falsehood personified (9.18).

The problem of contradiction that I have placed at the heart of the gender discourse of the Hindus is thus dramatically illustrated by Manu. If we take all these comments to originate with the same person, then they become utterly incomprehensible in their inconsistency. That inconsistency can be explained away only by the assumption commonly made that it was *not* the same person who wrote these different judgements and that there was more than one Manu, each responsible for different parts of the total *ouevre*. Leaving aside this contentious claim, we can see how insistently the sanctions against women force their way to the forefront of the discourse, and with what increasing pace, as sociological thought expands and the scattered and incidental comments on women we find in the early texts coalesce into a discipline specifically focussed on women in the *smṛti* tradition. Much later, Tryambakayajvan, an eighteenth-century writer from Thanjavur, continues in a similar vein in his *Strīdharmapaddhati* to make degrading comments on women: '*nanu svabhavato duṣṭānāṃ strīṇāṃ nirupitadharmaśravaṇe ca kathaṃ pravṛttiḥ*' (the problem is [*nanu*], how can there be any [real] inclination towards receiving religious inclination . . . on the part of women who are by nature corrupt?) (Leslie 1995 [1989], p. 246, 21r.3).

Manu is not the only *smṛtikāra* who denies women independence. His declaration that a woman is under the dominion of her father in youth, her husband during marriage, and her son in her old age, and that she can never act on her own is anticipated by Vasiṣṭha (5.1; 5.3), Baudhāyana (2.3.44–5), and Gautama (18.1), and reiterated with little change by Yājñavalkya (1.85), Viṣṇu (25.12; 13), and Nārada (13.30–31). Kauṭilya, who acknowledges women as individuals and is the first ethicist to do so, nonetheless shares the same distrust of women's independence. He allows a widow to inherit her husband's property until she remarries (6.14.4), and yet agrees that women must remain subordinate to men. At the same time, many of these sages place women high on the chain of being. For example, Baudhāyana (2.4.4) and Vasiṣṭha (5.5; 28.4) assert that women are ever pure and free from the taints of the world because they purge impurities out of their bodies by means of their monthly period. Baudhāyana goes on to say that 'Somadeva made women sacred and *gandharvas* gave them a melodious voice; Agni made them delightful to everyone; therefore they are free from sin' (2.4.5). Even Manu believes that a woman's impurity is washed away by her monthly menstruation (5.108). But the general view is adverse and runs parallel to Manu in postulating women's nature as an exclusive category and in constructing it in terms of specific vices. For example, the Buddhist author, Aśvaghoṣa, proclaims in his *Saundarānanda*:

> 8.41: Just as a cow, if restrained from grazing in one object, goes straight to another, so a woman regardless of a former love, goes elsewhere to take her pleasure.
>
> 8.42: For women may mount their husbands' funeral pyre, they may follow them closely at risk of their lives, they may be subjected to no restraint, but they never bear love wholeheartedly.
>
> 8.43: Even those women who treat their husbands as gods and sometimes in one way or the other give them pleasure, from fickleness of mind please themselves a thousand times.[8]
>
> (Johnston, 1975 [1928], pp. 45–6)

The view of brutish lust that Manu and Aśvaghoṣa hold to be a defining characteristic of women is not shared by everyone, but the attribution of deceit, greed and vanity is common. The *Devībhāgavatapurāṇa* states that, 'Falsehood, vain boldness, craftiness, stupidity, impatience, over-greediness, impurity and harshness are the natural qualities of women' (1.5.83). The *Garuḍapurāṇa* warns that 'no confidence should be reposed in . . . women' (109, 14). Not surprisingly perhaps, in the opinion of the *Rāmāyaṇa*, women are unstable as lightning, they are like the sharp edge of a sword, unsettled as the blast of a storm (*Araṇyakāṇḍa*, 13.5–6), fickle and cruel (*Araṇyakāṇḍa*, 45.29.30). The *Mahābhārata*, containing as it does many narratives of powerful, noble and self-sacrificing women, nevertheless opposes the independence of women (*Anuśāsanaparva*, 20.21), and later advises that there is 'nothing more wicked than a woman; they are the edge of a razor, poison, snake and fire combined in one' (*Anuśāsanaparva*, 38.12; 29), and that 'women's nature is inherently uncontrollable' (*Anuśāsanaparva*, 38.16). Then again in the *Śāntiparva* a woman's position is held to be exalted only when she is a wife (*Śāntiparva*, 144.16–17).

The distrust of women and their subjection to male relatives increasingly restrict their lives within domestic roles, which, in the absence of any other viable model, are necessarily exalted as vehicles of virtue. Since to be born as a girl child was a misfortune, some categories of female identity were needed to countervail the disadvantages of that burden, and these were found in the roles, indispensable for biological as much as social reasons, of mother and wife. These identities therefore occupied the foreground of public consciousness if we are to judge by the emphasis on them in legal, ethical and literary texts. The reverence for motherhood was no doubt facilitated by the powerful goddess cults but it also tied in with the need to ensure patrilinear continuity. It was therefore essential to extol wifehood for the obvious reason that a good wife was one who had borne or would bear sons. Yājñavalkya regards the mother as the highest of all (1.35), and all *smṛtikāras* agree in conferring the highest status in all relationships upon the mother, placing a mother even above the *guru* and the father. A father might be ostracized on committing impure acts, but a mother could never be abandoned. Baudhāyana and Āpastamba advise young initiates that after *upanayana*, their first alms must be taken from their mothers. Śankha-likhita goes to the length of declaring that in a dispute a son should side with the mother rather than with the father.

As I have noted above, the exaltation of the mother was correlated with the tradition of goddess worship. That tradition acquired particular force and currency with the advent of *tāntrism*, which, by recognizing the mystic power of the female, was undoubtedly instrumental in elevating the idea of womanhood and thereby of motherhood. The *Mahānirvāṇatantra* declares, 'Every woman, O Goddess, is your very form, your body concealed within the universe' (10.80) and in the same vein the *Śaktisaṅgamatantra* says, 'Woman is the creator of the universe; the universe is her form. Woman is the foundation of the world' (2.13). The *Kulārṇavatantra* makes the equation even more explicit when it says that 'every woman is born into the family (*kula*) of the Great Mother' (11.64).

This reverence for the mother remains constant through the discourse on women but attention turns more to the role of the wife the closer we get to modern times. In treatises on conduct appear innumerable comments on the felicity of wifehood and wifely duty, often coupled with instructive examples. A particularly exalted portrayal of womanhood as wifehood appears in the *Śāntiparva* (144.16–17) of the *Mahābhārata*. The burden of wifely duty becomes increasingly heavier and its rewards, always in terms of reputation and always to be gained in the next world, increasingly come to be contingent upon absolute and unquestioning service to the husband. This course is enjoined upon wives, to the exclusion of all others, given the all-absorbing demands of unlimited service, by all arbiters of conduct, such as, Manu, Bṛhaspati, Yājñavalkya, Vyāsa, Śankha-likhita,

Devala, Ṛṣyaśṛṅga, Kātyāyana, the collection known as *Smṛticandrikā* (*Vyavahārakhaṇḍa*). All advise women to commit themselves to household duties and to serve their husbands without question, and all promise that thereby good wives will attain heaven.

Even motherhood is subsumed within wifely duty as the demand upon the wife to produce sons becomes insistent. Total surrender to the husband's interests, which includes the duty of bearing his children – and male children at that – becomes the validation of wifely existence. The *Brahmavaivartapurāṇa* declares that the life of a woman who has no son is useless (2.16). Men need wives for procreative purposes, as we find in the popular (though unattributed) dictum, '*putrārthe kriyate bhāryā*', and Nārada explicitly says that '*apatyārthaṃ striyaḥ sṛṣṭāḥ . . .*' (12.19), that is, women are created to bring forth sons. Nārada admonishes husbands to consort only with wives who have brought forth male children, '*striyaṃ putravatīṃ vandyām . . .*' (12.83), and never with barren women, nor with those who give birth to daughters, '*bandhyām strījananīm nindyāṃ pratikūlāṃ ca sarvadā . . .*' (12.94). Sexual morality is a flexible value for Nārada, who allows intercourse with wanton women (*svairiṇī*), prostitutes (*veśyā*), and female slaves (*dāsī*) (12.78), who are presumably not covered by the injunction on men to protect women.

It is not that some reservations are not sounded in spelling out wifely duty but the general requirement of obedience stands. Typically, the material from Manu is self-contradictory, even more drastically than in the passages we have noted earlier. In 5.153 Manu says a husband of vile character must not be served until he is purified. But in the very next verse (5.154) he declares that no matter how vicious the husband, he must be served unquestioningly by a virtuous wife, for he is her god. The more balanced and less opinionated Yājñavalkya believes that if a husband is guilty of a heinous crime, he must not be served (1.77). But wifely submission is nevertheless a given of social and personal relations, to which women are allowed no alternative, and their lives become increasingly constricted within wifehood as time goes by. *Pātivrātya* is a constant theme in the *Padmapurāṇa*, which reiterates its value in three of its seven parts, the *sṛṣti*, *bhūmi*, and *uttara khaṇḍas*.

The regulations governing a wife's existence reach an unprecedented elaboration in the eighteenth century with Tryambaka, whose *Strīdharmapaddhati* is a manual that sets down in detail the daily routine that the ideal wife must follow.[9] The rules are too many and too complicated to report but the principles that underpin them are clear. Women are sometimes viewed as fundamentally impure by reason of their unavoidable condition of menstruation (*Strī.Dh.Pa.* 33v.8–40r.3, pp. 283–8), a view that totally reverses the *tāntric* dictum that it is that very discharge of blood that proves the inalienable purity of women, as stated, for instance in the *Jñānarṇavatantra* (22.26–31). Although Tryambaka quotes the views of various scholars, such as Baudhāyana, Vasiṣṭha and Yājnavalkya, who see women as the purest beings cleansed by their monthly menstruation, in his own view, on the contrary, we may see the culmination of centuries of assertions of women's fundamental *impurity*. Many writers firmly believed in this impurity in women,[10] a position maintained by some even today. The primary religious duty of a wife is obedient service to her husband, which she must carry out without regard even to the saving of her own life. More interestingly still, she is required to serve her husband even when it conflicts with other duties, which is a requirement that in effect isolates her from the public world by alienating her from its rules and principles. Following upon this abandonment of principles, the virtuous wife must abdicate her individuality and her principles so entirely that she must accept her husband's action even of selling her, for which there is of course the precedence of King Hariścandra's sale of his queen Śaibyā in the *Mārkaṇḍeyapurāṇa*.

What such precepts and examples imply is a wholesale depersonalization of women. The individual character of a woman becomes irrelevant when the female sex is forced into the mould of wifely duty and of virtue understood as chastity, of which a tragic example is Sītā's banishment by Rāma. A wife is an ever-ready servant on the one hand and an item of property. What is more, she is not property merely as social capital in the sense of securing for her husband prestige through her exemplary service and unsullied reputation. In a potently economic sense, she is also an investment as the producer of male offspring through whom alone a secure and prosperous future may be realized. The wife being a mere instrument in this project, her mental or moral constitution becomes meaningless, and as a result, her personhood.

If women's mental and moral attributes were irrelevant, what social standing might they have? Surprisingly, against the background sketched above, the authorities are most considerate about enabling women economically. Although the issue of women's paid labour seems beyond anyone's imagination, which leaves that part of women's possible economic profile blank, women's right of inheritance and their right to possess wealth are extensively and carefully discussed by Manu (9.118; 194), Yājñavalkya (2.115; 123; 124; 135; 143), Nārada (13.8), Devaṇabhaṭṭa (*Smṛti Candrikā*, p. 657), Bṛhaspati (*Bṛhaspati Smṛti*, 26.92, 93), Kātyāyana (*Kātyāyana Smṛti Sāroddhāra*, 894), Kauṭilya and many others. A woman's wealth is known as *strīdhana*.[11] That wealth may be of various types depending on its origin, as for instance:

adhyāgni (property given to the bride in front of the [wedding] fire), *adhyāvāhanika* (gift received by a bride on the way to her husband's home), *prītidatta* (gifts given with affection), *anvādheya* (gifts given subsequently by her kinsmen and in-law's family), *saudāyika* (gifts given by parental family), *ādhivedanika* (gifts given to the first wife), *yautaka* (dowry), *śulka* (bride-price) and *vṛtti* (subsistence). These were considered to be the types of wealth over which a woman had sole right. Many writers debated the husband's right to his wife's property without resolving the issue but most agreed that women had exclusive rights to their personal wealth. That women's right to personal wealth was universally acknowledged is attested in two of the best-known classical Sanskrit plays. When Vasantasenā's necklace is stolen and suspicion falls on Cārudatta, his wife offers her own necklace to save her husband's honour both in Bhāsa's *Cārudattam* (prose portion after verse 15, act 3) and in Śūdraka's *Mṛcchakaṭikam* (prose portion after verse 26, act 3). In both plays Cārudatta refuses (*Cārudattam,* 3.17; *Mṛcchakaṭikam.* 3, p. 196), as according to the laws of the time he should, as an honourable man. However, she gives it to him anyway, pointing out that as the necklace came from her family, it is her *strīdhana,* that is, her very own property to do with it whatever she wishes. The possession of personal wealth lent women a measure of influence in their personal lives. That women were accorded some authority and power even within their circumscribed sphere appears in several plays by Kalidāsa,[12] although, as Stephanie Jamison has remarked, they do not show 'feminist empowerment'. However, in continuation Jamison points out that women's portrayal in such narratives does indicate the acknowledgment of women's authority as they 'show some thematic complexes in early Indian traditions and some ritual roles in earlier traditions played by women'.[13]

If the right of ownership was vital to women's well-being, their right of remarriage was no less so. Since the early writers provided for women's rights to personal wealth, and the dramatists provided platforms for women to voice their opinions on that right, we may go farther and ask what views were held regarding women's right to remarry. The issue, which concerned a woman's fundamental rights as an individual, was addressed often and generated a great deal of controversy through history from the ancient to the medieval period, continuing in modern times as a legal question till legislation accorded that right in the 1950s. How universally the right has been accepted in social practice is yet to be seen. Here I shall trace the controversy briefly through time, beginning with the Vedic era.

The remarriage of women was not unknown in Vedic times. The term *punarbhū,* meaning a remarried woman, appears as early as in the

Atharvaveda (9.5.27–8). *Smṛtikāra* Baudhāyana prescribes remarriage for a woman whose husband is impotent, rendered outcaste, or dead (2.3.27; 4.1.16). Vasiṣṭha adds one more condition by advising that if the husband becomes insane, a woman is allowed to remarry (17.20). Manu refers to *paunarbhava* sons, that is, sons of a remarried woman, indicating that the remarriage of a woman under some conditions was in practice. However, he never encourages women's remarriage, saying that for a chaste woman (*sādhvī*) remarriage is inadvisable (5.160). Obviously, he himself disapproves of remarriage. Nārada (12.46–8) refers to three types of remarriages. Yājñavalkya (1.67) and Viṣṇu (15.8) also refer to *punarbhū*. Parāśara sounds a stronger note when he allows a woman to remarry in five situations of crisis, namely, her husband's disappearance, death, renunciation of the world, impotence and the loss of caste (4.28). The same verse reappears in *Garuḍapurāṇa* (107.8), which ascribes it to Parāśara. Nārada again repeats the same verse (12.97). Some later writers claimed Manu and Bṛhaspati to be authors of the verse but the verse does not appear in their work. Given the prestige and authority of legendary sages, this verse understandably created a great deal of controversy over the issue because society at large never felt comfortable with the idea of remarriage of women but could not dismiss the opinion of such esteemed personages lightly. At any rate, the citations given above suggest that the *dharmaśāstras* and *smṛti* texts by and large approved the remarriage of women. The practice was unquestionably embedded in the traditions of Hindu society.

Why and when, then, was the right to remarry taken away from women? Manu's writings show the sign of his uneasiness over women's remarriage in the fifth chapter of his *Manusmṛti* (5.160), as we have already noted. If he says, 'chaste women do not remarry', it becomes very difficult to overcome that daunting injunction. It is true that he refers to *punarbhū* (remarried woman) while referring to a *paunarbhava* son, that is, the son of a *punarbhū*, implicitly acknowledging the existence of a remarried woman as a social reality, but very reluctantly, and never prescribes remarriage in any of his verses. Other *smṛtikāras* modify the injunction by saying that it has to be understood that the first marriage has not been consummated when a woman is allowed to remarry. Some argue that remarriage is not allowed for a woman in the Kali age. Some have also argued for the custom of *niyoga* or levirate when the husband dies without leaving a son.[14] It is Medhatithi, the influential tenth-century commentator on Manu, who emphatically denies women this right by reinterpreting the term '*pati*' as a woman's protector (*pālanāt patim* . . .) in general rather than in the specific sense of a husband.[15] Taken in this broad sense, a woman's '*pati*' could be any guardian within the family. If the woman does not have a proper guardian in her own family, the king can be the *pālaka pati* or the protector. By Medhātithi's time, Parāśara's argument for allowing women to remarry was perhaps gaining the approval of many *smṛtikāras* who agreed with his view. But with Medhātithi's interpretation, which suited many orthodox schools, gradually the liberal views were submerged under orthodox and patriarchal voices. Commentators on Manu, Gautama, Yājñavalkya or Parāśara, such as Maskari (approximately tenth–eleventh century), Devaṇabhaṭṭa (approximately twelfth century), Nandapaṇḍita (approximately sixteenth century) and Bālambhaṭṭa (late eighteenth and early nineteenth century), among many others, follow in the footsteps of Medhātithi.

I may mention in this context an intriguing idea correlating the law and social practice that continually occurs in the writings of the *smṛtikāras*, including in their discussion of women's remarriage. This idea, stated unambiguously by Nārada, is that social custom is more powerful than normative ideals and that *dharma* or religious injunction is overruled by custom (*vyāvahāra hi valavān dharmas tena avahīyate* (*Nāradasmṛti*, 1.40). Many *smṛtikāras* repeat the same sentiment, advising that when in doubt, one ought to follow the custom of society and not *śāstra*. This would argue for the retention of the ancient acceptance of women's remarriage, but history shows orthodoxy's triumph over the pragmatism enjoined by Baudhāyana, Vasiṣṭha, Yājñavalkya, Parāśara, Nārada and others.

Through the ages the orthodox view prevailed and the remarriage even of young widows became a cherished taboo for Hindu society, unchallenged till the mid-1800s when Pandit Ishwarchandra Vidyasagar waged a virtually one-man crusade for the social acceptance of the remarriage of widows and 'placed a petition before the Legislative Council, along with a draft bill that passed on July 26, 1856, legalizing the remarriage of Hindu widows'.[16] This was the Widow Remarriage Act XV of 1856, which allowed only widows to remarry. Finally, a hundred years later, in 1956, through the Hindu Marriage Act women regained what they had once they had, at least partially, that is, equal rights with men to remarry and divorce.

Looking over the centuries of ethical and literary commentary on women, one is struck by the continuing derogation of women's fundamental traits and the increasing hardening of the boundaries set on women's life, as also by the unceasingly disputatious nature of the discourse. But beyond that, it is important to recognize the numerous questions a modern observer is driven to ask, none of which has a ready answer. The most puzzling is, why would an ideology that placed femininity at the very centre of its spiritual foundation view women with systematic disdain? As recounted in the survey offered here, throughout the history of Hindu society countless authorities have argued otherwise. Obviously, their voices were not loud enough to arrest the process of reducing women to second-class status or worse, a process facilitated by an ideological rhetoric that made women's disempowerment palatable and even desirable in women's self-fashioning.

The material relating to gender issues outlined here points to that historical process as one of subordinating the lives of one section of the body politic to the survival and advancement of the aggregate. The mechanism of that process has been one of formulating a serviceable ideology whereby the sacrificial victims have been persuaded not only to consent to their own victimhood but actually to applaud it. The most dramatic example of that mechanism of making the victim welcome their oppression is the institution of *satī*. The ideology enforcing this and other demands upon women operates particularly powerfully in the textual mode because of the enduring authority of the written word. It is through textual practice that an idealized and essentialized persona for women is fashioned, comprising character traits that exclusively serve specific gender interests in a social organization geared best to serve the economic and political needs of particular historical times. The expanse and diversity of the textual construction of women will be evident from the material gathered in the following section.

SECTION 2: SELECTED TEXTUAL PASSAGES WITH TRANSLATIONS*

(1) On the birth of a daughter

(a) Unsympathetic views

Atharvaveda

prajāpatir anumatiḥ sinīvālya acīklṛpat |
straiṣūyam anyatra dadhat pumāṃsam uṃ dadhad iha | |

(*Atharvaveda*, 6.11.3)

* Unless otherwise indicated, translations are mine. The examples offered here represent only a part of the vast textual material available but they give us a fair idea of the nature of society's approach towards women.

The Lord of creatures [gives] consent and active life (*sinivālī*) to shape the embryo. May they place a male here and the birth of a girl elsewhere.

yaṃ parihastam abibhar aditiḥ putrakāmyā tvaṣṭā |
tam asyā ā badhnād yathā putram janād iti | |
(*Atharvaveda*, 6.81.3)

The bangle that Aditi wore, with the desire of [bearing] a son – the universal architect has bound the same [bangle] on this woman, so that she may bear a son.

Taittirīya Saṃhitā

. . . *striyaṃ jātām parāsyantyut pumāṃsaṃ haranti* . . .
(*Taittirīya Samhitā*, 6.5.10.38)

. . . abandons the girl child in case one is robbed of a son . . .

Aitareya Brāhmaṇa

annaṃ ha prāṇaḥ śaraṇaṃ ha vāso rūpaṃ hiraṇyaṃ paśavo vivāhāḥ |
sakhā ha jāyā kṛpaṇaṃ ha duhitā jyotir ha putraḥ parame vyoman | |
(*Aitareya Brāhmaṇa*, 3.33.1)

Food is life, clothing is protection, gold is beauty, marriage is for men. [One's] Wife is a friend, a daughter is misery and a son is the light in the highest heaven.

[Another dictum is cited by Sāyanācārya as a comment on this verse:]

sambhave svajanaduḥkhakārikā sampradānasamaye'rthahārikā |
yauvane'pi bahudoṣakārikā dārikā hṛdayadārikā pituḥ | |
(*Aitareya Brāhmaṇa*, 1991, p. 229)

At birth [a girl] creates pain for her father [lit: relatives], [she] takes away [his] wealth at the time of *sampradāna* [marriage] in her youth [she] makes too many misadventures [lit: mistakes]. A daughter breaks her father's heart.

Manusmṛti

. . . duhitā kṛpaṇaṃ param |

(*Manusmṛti*, 4.185)

. . . a daughter is the ultimate object of pity.

The *Mahābhārata*[17]

. . . kṛcchaṃ tu duhitā kila

(*Mbh, Ādiparva*, 147.11)

. . . a daughter is indeed misery [for parents].

mātuḥ kulaṃ pitṛkulaṃ yatra caiva pradīyate |
kulatrayaṃ saṃśayituṃ kurute kanyakā satām | |

(*Mbh, Udyogaparva*, 95.16)

A daughter creates difficulties in all three families, of mother, father and in the family to which she is given away.

The *Rāmāyaṇa*

kanyāpitṛtvaṃ duḥkhaṃ hi sarveṣāṃ mānakāṅkṣiṇām |
na jñāyate ca kaḥ kanyāṃ varayed iti kanyake | |

(*Rām, Uttarakāṇḍa*, 9.9)

Being the father of a daughter is misery to everyone who desires honour. No one knows who will wed the daughter.

(b) Celebrating the birth of a son

ṚgVeda

putraṃ prāvargaṃ kṛṇute suvīrye dāśnoti nama uktibhiḥ |

(*ṚV.*, 8, 4.6b)

[O Indra!] Whoever bows and recites this [prayer] gains a handsome and brave son, destroyer of enemies.

Bṛhadārṇyaka Upaniṣad

. . . aṅgād aṅgāt sambhavasi hṛdayād adhijāyase . . .

(*Bṛ.Upa.*, 6.4.9)

. . . Thou that from every limb art come,
That from the heart thou art generate . . .

(E. Roer, 2000, pp. 440–1)

[There is no indication whether the child mentioned is a boy or a girl. The same verse is cited by Bṛhaspati to assert the equivalence of sons and daughter.]

Baudhāyana Dharmasūtra

aṅgād aṅgāt saṃbhavasi hṛdayād adhijāyase ।
ātmā vai putra nāmāsi sa jīva śaradaḥ śatam iti । ।

(*Bau.Dh.Sū.*, 2.3.14)

From my limb to limb you are born! From my heart you take life! You are my very own self, bearing the name 'son'. May you live a hundred autumns!

The *Mahābhārata*

ātmā putraḥ sakhā bhāryā . . .

(*Mbh, Ādiparva*, 147.11)

A son is one's own self, a wife is a friend . . .

Nāradasmṛti

bandhyāṃ strījananīṃ nindyāṃ pratikūlāṃ ca sarvadā ।
kāmatī nābhinandeta kurvannevaṃ sa doṣabhāk ।

(*Nāradasmṛti*, 12.94)

Let not a husband show love to a barren woman, or to one who gives birth to female children only, or whose conduct is blamable, or who constantly contradicts him; if he does (have conjugal intercourse with her), he becomes liable to censure (himself).

(Jolly 1988 [1889], p. 184)

Brahmavaivartapurāṇa

yā strī putravihīnā ca jīvanaṃ tannirarthakam । ।

(*Brahmavaivartapurāṇa, Gaṇapati Khaṇḍa*, 46.21)

The life of a woman who has no son is useless.

(c) Sympathetic views

The *Matsyapurāṇa*

yad arthaṃ duhitur janma necchanty api mahāphalam

(*Matsyapurāṇa*, 154.414)

Even when the birth of a daughter is unwelcome, it earns high merit.

. . . śāstreṣu uktam asandigdhaṃ bahuvāraṃ mahāphalam | *daśaputrasamā kanyā . . .*

(*Matsyapurāṇa*, 154.157)

All that has been stated in the *śāstras* is quite true [beyond doubt]. The *karmas* yielding great fruits are repeated often. In the *śāstras*, at many places it has been said, a girl is equal to ten sons.

(d) Affection for a daughter

The *Mahābhārata*

manyate kecid adhikaṃ snehaṃ putre pitur narāḥ |
kanyāyāṃ naiva tu punar mama tulyāv ubhau matau | |

(*Mbh, Ādiparva*, 145.36)

Some fathers love their sons more, some [love] their daughters [more]. For me, both are equal [as my affection goes].

The *Matsyapurāṇa*

tato gate bhagavati nīlalohite sahomayā ratim alabhanna bhūdharaḥ |
sabāndhavo bhavati ca kasya no mano vihvalañca jagati hi kanyakāpituḥ | |

(*Matsyapurāṇa*, 154.497)

After the departure of Nīlalohita with Umā, the king [Himācala] felt very lonely [lit: not having] and agitated [in the absence of Pārvatī] as is often the case in this world when the father [sees] the daughter [departing after marriage].

Abhijñānaśakuntalam

yāsyatyadya śakuntaleti hṛdayaṃ samspṛṣṭam utkaṇṭhayā
kaṇṭhaḥ stambhitabāṣpavṛttikaluṣaś cintājaḍaṃ darśanam |

vaiklavyaṃ mama tāvad īdṛśam idaṃ snehād araṇyaukasaḥ
pīḍyante gṛhiṇaḥ kathaṃ nu tanayāviśleṣaduḥkhair navaiḥ । ।
(*Abhijñānaśakuntalam*, Act 4.6)

My heart is touched with sadness
since Śakuntalā must go today,
my heart is choked with sobs,
my eyes are dulled by worry –
if a disciplined ascetic
suffers so deeply from love,
how do fathers bear the pain
of each daughter's parting?

(Miller 1984, p. 126)

Harṣacarita

[At the thought of Rājyaśrī's marriage Grahavarmā laments to his queen Yaśomatī his sadness at having to give his daughter away:]

udvegamahāvarte pātayati . . . ।
saridiva taṭam anuvarṣaṃ vivardhamānā sutā pitaram । ।
(*Harṣacarita*, Act 4, verse 5)

A growing daughter causes a whirlpool of anxiety for her father like a whirlpool by a riverbank.

. . . *apatyatve samāne api jātāyāṃ duhitari dūyante santaḥ* ।
(*Harṣacarita*, Act 4, prose portion after verse 5)

Good men feel sad at the birth of their daughter, though both [son and a daughter] are equally their offspring.

[The queen expresses her feelings by saying:]

kevalaṃ kṛpākṛtaviśeṣaḥ sudūreṇa tanayasnehād atiricyate duhitṛsnehaḥ ।
(*Harṣacarita*, Act 4, prose portion after verse 5)

Love for her daughter more than her son is generated out of pity [since she has to be given away in marriage].

. . . *duhitṛsnehkātaratarahṛdayā*. . . .
(*Harṣacarita*, Act 4. prose portion after verse 5)

. . . whose heart feels extreme pain out of affection for her daughter . . .

(2) On the essential nature of women

ṚgVeda

. . . striyāḥ aśāsyaṃ manaḥ | uto aha kratuṃ raghum |

(*ṚV.*, 8.33.17)

The mind of women brooks no discipline. Her intellect has little weight.

na vai straiṇāni sakhyāni santi sālāvṛkāṇām hṛdayāṇyetā |

(*ṚV.*, 10, 95.15)

With women there can be no friendship. Women's hearts are like those of hyenas.

Śatapatha Brāhmaṇa

anṛtam strī śudraḥ śvā kṛṣṇah śakunis . . .

(*Śatapatha Brāhmaṇa*, 14.1.1.31)

A woman, a *śudra*, a dog and a crow are the embodiments of untruth, sin and darkness.

(Leslie 1995 [1989], p. 251)

Manusmṛti

svabhāva eṣa nārīṇāṃ narāṇām iha dūṣaṇam |
ato arthān na pramādyanti pramadāsu vipaścitaḥ | |

(*Manusmṛti*, 2.213)

To corrupt men in the world is women's essential nature. Therefore, wise men do not heedlessly seek pleasure among wanton women.

evaṃ svabhāvaṃ jñātvā āsāṃ prajāpatinisargajam |
paramaṃ yatnam ātiṣṭhet puruṣo rakṣaṇaṃ prati | |
śayyāsanam alaṃkāraṃ kāmaṃ krodham anāryatām |
dogdhṛbhāvaṃ kucaryāṃ ca strībhyo manur akalpayet | |
nāsti strīṇāṃ kriyā mantrair iti dharme vyāvasthitiḥ |
nirindriyā hyamantrāś ca strīyo anṛtam iti sthitiḥ | |

(*Manusmṛti*, 9.16–18)

[The translation of this passage appears in section 1 of this chapter.]

The *Mahābhārata*

na strībhyaḥ kiñcid anyad vai pāpīyastaram asti vai ǀ
striyo hi mūlam doṣāṇām tathā tvam api vettha ha ǀ ǀ
(*Mbh, Anuśāsanaparva*, 38.12)

There is no one viler than a woman. A woman is the root cause of all evil, you must know that.

[Verses 15–20 of chapter 38 again elaborate on the inherently vile nature of women. Here I give only one example from this group.]

anarthitvāt manuṣyāṇāṃ bhayāt parijanasya ca ǀ
maryādāyām amaryādāḥ strīyas tiṣṭhanti bhartṛṣu ǀ ǀ
(*Mbh, Anuśāsanaparva*, 38.16)

Women have no sense of *maryādā* or morality and propriety. She abides in *maryādā* out of fear of people and her relatives around her, and her husband beside her can make her [abide in *maryādā*].

antakaḥ śamano mṛtyuḥ pātālaṃ vaḍavāmukham ǀ
kṣuradhārā viṣaṃ sarpo bahnir ekataḥ striyaḥ ǀ ǀ
(*Mbh, Anuśāsanaparva*, 38.29)

Yama, destroyer, death, hell, entrance to the lower regions, the edge of a sword, poison and fire – a woman is a combination of all of that.

na ca strīṇām kriyā kācid iti dharmo vyavasthitaḥ ǀ
nirindriyā amantrāś ca striyo anṛtam iti śrutiḥ ǀ ǀ
(*Mbh, Anuśāsanaparva*, 40.11–12)

Women do not act according to *dharma*. They have no control over their sense organs, they do not have [any knowledge of] *mantras*. Women live [their lives] in falsehood.

The *Rāmāyaṇa*

śatahṛdānāṃ lolotvaṃ śastrāṇāṃ tīkṣṇatāṃ tathā ǀ
garuḍānilayoḥ śaighryam anugacchanti yoṣitaḥ ǀ ǀ
(*Rām, Araṇyakāṇḍa*, 13.6)

Women are quick as lightning [in severing a relationship], sharp as weapons [in cutting off a friendship] and [create mischief] at the speed of Garuḍa's [flight] and the wind.

svabhāvastv eṣa nārīṇām eṣu lokeṣu dṛśyate ।
vimuktadharmāś capalās tīkṣṇā bhedakarāḥ striyaḥ । ।
(*Rām, Araṇyakāṇḍa*, 45.29–30)

Such is the nature of women as can be seen in the world. Women are [usually] careless about *dharma*, they are fickle-minded, sharp [tongued] and they betray [friends].

Pañcatantra

anṛtaṃ sāhasaṃ māyā mūrkhatvam atilobhitā ।
aśaucaṃ nirdayatvañca strīṇāṃ doṣā svabhāvajāḥ । ।
(*Pañcatantra, Mitrabheda*, 207)

Falsehood, aggression, deception, ignorance, greed, impurity, cruelty are flaws natural to women.

Saundarānanda

viṣayād viṣayāntaraṃ gatā pracaraty eva yathā hṛtāpi gauḥ ।
anavekṣitapūrvasauhṛdā ramate 'nyatra gatā tathāṅganā । ।
praviśyantyapi hi striyaś citām anubadhnyanty api muktajīvitāḥ ।
api bibhrati naiva yantraṇā na tu bhāvena vahanti sauhṛdam । ।
ramayanti patīn kathañcana pramadā yāḥ patidevatāḥ kvacit ।
calccittatayā sahasraśo ramayante hṛdayaṃ svam eva tāḥ । ।
(*Saundarānanda*, 8.41–3)

[The translation of this passage is included in the body of the text in section 1 of this chapter.]

Garuḍapurāṇa

nādīnāṃ ca nakhīnāṃ ca śṛṅgīnāṃ śastrapāṇinām ।
viśvāso naiva gantavyaḥ strīṣu rājakuleṣu ca । ।
(*Garuḍapurāṇa*, 109.14)

Rivers, animals with nails and horns, [human beings] with weapons in hands, women and members of the royal family are never to be trusted.

Devībhāgavatapurāṇa

anṛtaṃ sāhasaṃ māyā mūrkhatvam atilobhatā ।
aśaucaṃ nirdayatvaṃ strīṇāṃ doṣāḥ svabhavajāḥ । ।.
(*Devībhāgavatapurāṇa*, 1.5.83)

Falsehood, vain boldness, craftiness, stupidity, impatience, overgreediness, impurity and harshness are natural attributes of women.

Strīdharmapaddhati

. . . svabhāvato duṣṭānām strīṇām . . .
calasvabhāvā duḥsevyā durgrāhyā bhāvatas tathā |
prajñāsya puruṣasyeha yathā vācas tathā striyaḥ | |

(*Strī.Dh.Pa.*, 21r.3; 21r.4–5)

. . . women are by nature corrupt . . .
[Women are] inherently fickle, difficult to manage, and in their very nature difficult to understand; as (unintelligible as) the words of a wise man, so are women.

(Leslie 1995 [1989], pp. 246–7)

(3) On the independence of women

Gautama Dharmasūtra

asvatantrā dharme strī | *nāticared bhartāram* | *vāk cakṣuḥ karmasamyatā* | |

(*Gau.Dh.Sū.*, 18.1–3)

A wife cannot act independently in matters relating to law. She should never go against her husband and keep her speech, her eyes and actions under strict control.

(Olivelle 2000, p. 167)

Baudhāyana Dharmasūtra

na striyāḥ svātantryaṃ vidyate | | *athāpy udāharanti* |
pitā rakṣati kaumāre bhartā rakṣati yauvane |
putras tu sthāvirībhāve na strī svātantryam arhati iti | |

(*Bau.Dh.Sū.*, 2.3.44–5)

There is no independence for women. Now, they also cite: Her father protects her in her childhood, her husband guards her in her youth, and her son takes care of her in her old age. A woman never gains independence.

Viṣṇusmṛti

sarvakarmasu asvantratā | |

(*Viṣṇusmṛti*, 25.12)

[A woman should not be] independent in all [her] actions.

bālyayauvanavārdhakyeṣv api pitṛbhartṛputrādhīnatā | |

(*Viṣṇusmṛti*, 25.13)

A woman should be dependent on her father, husband and son, in her childhood, youth and old age.

Vasiṣṭha Dharmasūtra

asvatantrā strī puruṣapradhānā |
pitā rakṣati kaumāre bhartā rakṣati yauvane |
putraś ca sthavire bhāve na strī svātantryamarhati iti |

(*Va.Dh.Sū.*, 5.1; 5.3)

Never independent, a woman is under male authority.
Her father protects her in her childhood, her husband guards her in her youth, and her son takes care of her in her old age. A woman never gains independence.

Manusmṛti

vālayā vā yuvatyā vā vṛdhyayā vāpi yoṣitā |
na svātantryeṇa kartvyaṃ kiñcit kāryaṃ gṛheṣv api | |
vālye piturvaśe tiṣṭhet pāṇigrāhasya yauvane |
putrāṇāṃ bhartari prete na bhajet strī svatantratām | |
pitrā bhartā sutair vāpi necched viraham ātmanaḥ |
eṣāṃ hi viraheṇa strī garhye kuryād ubhe kule | |

(*Manusmṛti*, 5.145–7)

A girl, a young woman, or even an old woman should not do anything independently, even (in her own) house.

In childhood a woman should be under her father's control, in youth under her husband's, and when her husband is dead, under her sons'. She should not have independence.

A woman should not try to separate herself from her father, her husband, or her sons, for her separation from them would make both (her own and her husband's) families contemptible.

(Doniger and Smith 1991, p.115)

asvatantrā striyaḥ kāryāḥ puruṣaiḥ svair divāniśam |
viṣayeṣu ca sajjantyaḥ saṃsthāpyā ātmano vaśe | |
pitā rakṣati kaumāre bhartā rakṣati yauvane |
rakṣanti sthavire putrā na strī svātantryam arhati | |

(*Manusmṛti*, 9.2–3)

Women, who are attached to material things, are to be kept dependent day or night by men and kept under their own control.

Her father protects her in childhood, her husband watches over her in youth, her sons maintain her in old age. A woman never gains independence.

Nāradasmṛti

svātantryād vipraṇaśyanti kule jātā api striyaḥ |
asvātantryam atas tāsāṃ prajāpatir akalpayet | |
pitā rakṣati kaumāre bhartā rakṣati yauvane |
putrā sthavire bhāve na strī svātantryam arhati | |

(*Nāradasmṛti*, 13.30–31)

It is through independence women go to ruin though be born in a noble family; therefore, the Lord of creatures ordained dependence for them.

The father protects her during her childhood, her husband in her youth, her sons in her old age; a woman has no right to independence.

(Jolly 1876, p. 98)

Yājñavalkyasmṛti

rakṣet kanyāṃ pitā vinnāṃ patiḥ putrās tu vārdhake |
abhāve jñātayas teṣāṃ na svātantryaṃ kvacit striyāḥ | |

(*Yājñavalkyasmṛti*, 1.85)

A father protects his daughter [in her childhood], her husband when she is married, and her son in her old age. In their absence the relatives [should look after a woman]. A woman cannot have independence.

The *Mahābhārata*

pitā rakṣati kaumāre bhartā rakṣati yauvane |
putrā sthavirībhāve nāsti strīṇām svatantrata | |

(*Mbh*, *Anuśāsanaparva*, 21.19)

In her childhood her father protects her, her husband protects her in her youth and her son [protects her] in her old age. A woman has no independence.

[This verse occurs also in some Purānas, e.g., *Padmapurāṇa*.]

(4) On women's education

Bṛhadāraṇyaka Upaniṣad

The birth of a learned daughter (*paṇḍitā*):

> *atha ya icched duhitā me paṇḍitā jāyeta sarvam āyuriyāditi tilaudanaṃ pācayitvā sarpiśmantam aśnīyātām īśvarau janayitavai* |
>
> (*Bṛ.Upa.*, 6.4.17)

> Now, in case, one wishes 'That a learned daughter be born to me! that she may attain the full length of life!' – they two [the husband and wife] should have rice boiled with sesame seed and should eat with ghee butter. They two are likely to beget [her].
>
> (E. Roer 2000, p. 444)

Pāṇini

Female teachers:

> *upādhyāyā, upādhyāyī.*
>
> (*Aṣṭādhyāyī, Kāśikā*, 3.3.21; 4.1.49)

[Both words denote female teachers, as the words are formed with the suffixes *ṭāp* and *ṅiṣ*. Literally the words mean: students approaching teachers for instructions.]

> *ācāryā*
>
> (*Aṣṭādhyāyī, Kāśikā*, 4.1.49)

[A female teacher.]

Bṛhaddevatā

A list of scholarly women:

> *ghoṣā godhā viśvavārā apālopniṣan niṣat* |
> *brahmajāyā juhūr nāma agastasya svasāditi* | |
> *indrāṇī cendramātā ca saramā romaśorvaśī* |
> *lopāmudrā ca nadyaś ca yamī nārī ca śaśvatī* | |
> *śrīr lākṣā sārparājñī vāk śraddhā medhā ca dakṣiṇā* |
> *rātri sūryā ca sāvitrī brahmavādinya īritāḥ* | |
>
> (*Bṛhaddevatā*, 2.82–4)

The names of the *brahmavādinīs* are: Ghoṣā, Godhā, Viśvavārā, Apālā, Upniṣat, Niṣat, Juhū (wife of Brahmā), Sister of Agastya, Aditi, Indrāṇī, Mother of Indra, Saramā, Romaśā, Urvaśī, Lopāmudrā, Rivers, Yamī, Nārī, Śvaśvatī, Śrī, Lākṣā, Sārparājñī, Vāk, Śraddhā, Medhā, Dakṣiṇā, Rātri, Sūryā and Sāvitrī.

Bṛhadāraṇyaka Upaniṣad

Dialogue between Gārgī (a female scholar) and Yājñavalkya (a male scholar):

> . . . *kasmin nu khalu brahmalokā otāśca protāśceti sa hovāca gārgi mātiprākṣīr mā te mūrdhā vyapaptadanatipraśnyāṃ vai devatām atipṛcchasi gārgi mātiprākṣīr iti tato ha gārgī vācaknavy upararāma* ।
>
> (*Bṛ.Upa.*, 3.6.1)

> . . . 'On what then are woven and rewoven the worlds of Brahman?'. 'Gārgī,'said he, 'do not ask an improper question, in order that thy head many not drop down. Thou askest the deity which is not to be questioned. Do not question, O Gārgī. Thence Gārgī, the daughter of Vacaknu, became silent.'
>
> (E. Roer 2000, p. 280)

Dialogue between Maitryeī and Yājñavalkya (learned wife and husband):

> *maitreyīti hovāca yājñavalkya udyāsan vā are aham asmāt sthānad asmi hanta te anayā kātyāyanyā antaṃ karavāṇīti* ।
>
> *sā hovāca maitreyī yannu ma iyam bhagoḥ sarvā pṛthivī vittena pūrṇā syāt kathaṃ tena amṛtā syām iti neti hovāca yājñvalkyo yathaivopakaraṇavatām jīvitaṃ tathaiva te jīvitaṃ syād amṛtatvasya tu nāśāsti vitteneti* ।
>
> *sā hovāca maitreyī yenāhaṃ nāmṛtā syāṃ kim ahaṃ tena kuryāṃ yadeva bhagavān veda tadeva me bruhīti* ।
>
> *sa hovāca yājñavalkyaḥ priyā batāre naḥ satī priyaṃ bhāṣasa ehyāsva vyākhyāsyāmi te vyācakṣāṇasya tu me nididhyāsasveti* ।
>
> (*Bṛ.Upa.*, 2.4.1–4)

> Yājñavalkya spoke thus to Maitreyī: 'O Maitreyī, I wish to elevate myself [from a householder's life]; let me then divide [my property] between you and Kātyāyanī.'

Maitreyī said, 'Reverend One, if this world with all its wealth were mine, would I then become immortal?'. Yājñavalkya said, 'Your life would become that of the wealthy but by wealth you will never gain immortality.'

Maitreyī said, 'If I did not become immortal by it, of what use would wealth be to me? Tell me, Reverend One, of any [means of obtaining immortality] that you know.'

Yājñvalkya said, '[You were] dear to us before, [but what now] you say is dearer. Come, sit down; I will explain to you [the means of earning immortality]. Listen with care to understand my explanation.'

Smṛticandrikā

Women's education (refers to Brahmin women):

> *yattu hāritenoktam'dvividhā striyo brahmavādinyas sadyovadhvaś ca* ǀ *tatra brahmavādinīnām upanayanam agnīndhanaṃ vedādhyayanaṃ svagṛhe ca bhikṣācaryeti* ǀ ǀ *sadyobadhūnām copasthite vivāhe kathan cid upanayanamantraṃ kṛtvā vivāhaḥ kāryaḥ, iti.*
>
> (Kane, vol. 1, p. 132)

As Hārita said, there can be two types of women, *brahmavādinī* [learned] and *sadyavadhū* [housewife]. A *brahmavādinī* goes through the initiation ceremony, Vedic studies, fire rituals and [ritual] begging in her own home. For a *sadyavadhū*, the minimum ritual of *upanayana* with *mantra* is performed at the time of marriage.

(5) On inheritance

(a) Women's rights to property

ṚgVeda

> . . . *yathā dharmāṇi sanatā na dūduṣat* ǀ
>
> (*ṚV.*, 3.3.1)

Daughters have no shares in the father's property.

Āpastamba Dharmasūtra

. . . duhitā vā

(*Apa.Dh.Sū.*, 2.14.4)

Alternatively, the daughter [inherits the property].

(b) Same rights for a couple to property

jāyāpatyor na vibhāgo vidyate | pāṇigrahaṇāddhi sahatvaṃ karmsu | tathā puṇyaphaleṣu | dravyaparigraheṣu ca | na hi bhartur vipravāse naimittike dāne steyam upadiśanti |

(*Apa.Dh.Sū.*, 2.14.16–20)

Between husband and wife there is no division [of assets]. Since their marriage they are bonded in performing [religious] rites, as also in receiving rewards of their meritorious deeds and in acquiring wealth. Never is it considered theft for the wife to make a necessary gift during the husband's sojourn abroad.

kuṭumbinau dhanasyeśāte | tayor anumate 'nye 'pi taddhiteṣu varteran |
(*Apa.Dh.Sū.*, 2.29.3–4)

A couple jointly own property. With their permission others also may tend to it for their benefit.

Gautama Dharmasūtra

piṇḍagotrarṣisaṃbandhā rikthaṃ bhajeran strī cānapatyasya |
(*Gau.Dh.Sū.*, 28.21)

The estate of a man who dies sonless is shared by those related to him through ancestry, lineage, or a common seer and by his wife.
(Olivelle 2000, p. 187)

strīdhanaṃ duhitṛṇām aprattānām apratiṣṭhitānāṃ ca | bhaginīśulkaḥ sodaryāṇām ūrdhvaṃ mātuḥ | pūrvaṃ caike |

(*Gau.Dh.Sū.*, 28.24–6)

The wife's wealth passes to her unmarried and penurious daughters. A sister's dowry passes to her uterine brothers after her mother dies; some say, even before.

Bṛhaspatismṛti

aṅgād aṅgāt saṁbhavati putravat duhitā nṛṇām |
tasmāt pitṛdhanaṃ tv anyaḥ kathaṃ gṛhṇita mānavaḥ | |

(*Bṛhaspatismṛti*, 25.56)

A daughter is born from [the same] human bodies as is a son. Why then, should the father's wealth be taken (inherited) by another person?

(Aiyangar 1941, pp. 217–18)

Baudhāyana Dharmasūtra

nirindriyā hyadāyāś ca striyo matā iti śrutiḥ |

(*Bau.Dh.Sū.*, 2.3.46)

Women are considered to be devoid of strength and not to inherit property, (*Taittirīya Samhitā*, 6.5.8.2), says a Vedic text.

(Olivelle 2000, p. 255)

Arthaśāstra

kanyābhyaś ca prādānikam |

(*Arthaśāstra*, 3.5.21)

[Younger unmarried] daughters should be given wealth [at the time of their marriage].

dravyam aputrasya sodaryā bhrātaraḥ sahajīvino vā hareyuḥ kanyāś ca . . .

(*Arthaśāstra*, 3.5.9)

If one does not have a son, his own brothers or persons, who have been living with him, [can inherit] property. [In their absence] a daughter can also inherit [her father's wealth which she may need for her marriage].

mṛte bhartari dharmakāmā tadānīm evāsthāpyā ābharaṇaṃ śulkaśeṣaṃ ca labheta | *labdhā vā vindamānā savṛddhikam ubhayaṃ dāpyeta* |

(*Arthaśāstra*, 3.2.19–20)

When the husband dies, if the wife wants to live a *dhārmic* or religious life, she retains her jewellery and her dowry and also the balance of her *śulka* or money due to her. If after obtaining them, she decides to remarry, she has to return both with whatever she has gained since with interest on their value.

Yājñavalkyasmṛti

yadi kuryāt samān aṃśān patnyaḥ kāryāḥ samāṃśikāḥ |
na dattaṃ strīdhanaṃ yāsām bhartrā vā śvaśureṇa vā | |

(*Yājñavalkyasmṛti*, 2.115)

If the father gives equal shares [to his sons], then his wives too will be receiving similar shares, if separate *strīdhana* has not already been given to them by their husband or by their father-in-law.

. . . *pitur ūrdhvaṃ vibhajatāṃ mātāpy aṃśaṃ samaṃ haret* | |

(*Yājñavalkyasmṛti*, 2.123)

. . . while making the partition after the father's death the widowed mother will be entitled to an equal share with her sons.

asaṃskṛtās tu . . . bhaginyaś ca nijād aṃśād dattām aṃśaṃ tu turīyakam | |

(*Yājñavalkyasmṛti*, 2.124)

. . . unmarried [lit: uninitiated] sisters will get one fourth from each brother's share.

patnī duhitaraś caiva . . .

(*Yājñavalkyasmṛti*, 2.135)

[In case a man dies sonless] his wife and then the daughters also inherit his property.

(6) On 'appointed' daughter

Gautama Dharmasūtra

pitotsṛjet putrikām anapatyo agniṃ prajāpatiṃ ceṣṭvāsmadartham apatyam iti saṃvādya |

(*Gau.Dh.Sū.*, 28.18)

Saying '[Your] son is for my benefit', a father lacking a son should offer oblations to Agni and Prajāpati, and appoint his daughter.

Viṣṇusmṛti

atha dvādaśa putrā bhavanti | |
putrikāputras tṛtīyaḥ | |
yas tasyāḥ putraḥ sa me putro bhaved iti yā pitrā datta saḥ putrikā | |

(*Viṣṇusmṛti*, 15.1; 4; 5)

Now, there are twelve types of sons. The third [type] is the son of an appointed daughter, *putrikāputra*. She is known as an appointed daughter, who is given away by her father, saying, 'Her son will be my son.'

(*Viṣṇusmṛti*, 2006, p. 64)

Arthaśāstra

svayaṃ jātaḥ kṛtakṛyāyām aurasaḥ | *tena tulyaḥ putrikāputraḥ* |

(*Arthaśāstra*, 3.7.4–5)

A son begotten by a man [on his wife] after observing required rituals is known as *aurasa*. *Putrikāputra* has similar [status].

(7) On strīdhana (women's wealth)

Manusmṛti

svābhyaḥ svābhyas tu kanyābhyaḥ pradadyur bhrātaraḥ pṛthak |
svāt svād aṁśāc caturbhāgaṃ patitāḥ syuraditsavaḥ. | |

(*Manusmṛti*, 9.118)

The brothers should separately give their unmarried sisters something from their own portions, a quarter from each one's share. They fall [in society] if they do not.

adhyagnyadhyāvāhanikaṃ dattaṃ ca prītikarmaṇi |
bhrātṛmātṛpitṛprāptaṃ ṣadvidhaṃ strīdhanaṃ smṛtam | |

(*Manusmṛti*, 9.194)

A woman's property is traditionally regarded as of six sorts: what was given in front of the (marriage) fire, on the bridal procession, or as a token of affection, and what she got from her brother, mother or father.

(Doniger and Smith 1991, p. 219)

Arthaśāstra

śulkaṃ strīdhanam aśulkastrīdhanāyās tat pramāṇam |
ādhivedanikam anurūpām ca vṛttiṃ dattvā bahvīr api vindeta | |

(*Arthaśāstra*, 3.2.41)

Having given the necessary amount of *śulka* and property (*strīdhana*) even those women who have not received such things on the occasion of their marriage with him, and also having given his wives the proportionate compensation and an adequate subsistence (*vṛtti*) he may marry any number of women.

(Shamasastry 1967, pp. 176–7)

Nāradasmṛti

mātrā ca svadhanaṃ dattam . . .

(*Nāradasmṛti*, 13.7)

[When] the mother bestows a portion of her property . . .

adhyagnyadhyāvāhanikaṃ bhartugāmyaprajāsu tu | |
bhrātṛmātṛpitṛprāptaṃ ṣaḍvidhaṃ strīdhanaṃ smṛtam | |

(*Nāradasmṛti*, 13.8)

What (was given) in front of the nuptial fire, during the bridal procession, the husband's donation, and what she got from her brother, mother and father, that is called the six-fold property of a woman (*strīdhana*).

(Jolly 1988 [1889], p. 190)

Yājñavalkyasmṛti

pitṛmātṛpatibhrātṛdattam adhyagnyupāgatam |
ādhivedanikādyaṃ ca strīdhanaṃ parikirtītam | |
bandhudattaṃ tathā śulkam anvādheyakam eva ca |

(*Yājñavalkyasmṛti*, 2.143–4)

Gifts given by father, mother, husband and brother near the nuptial fire, [gifts] given as *adhivedana* [to the first wife at the time of the second marriage] are known as *strīdhana*.

[Gifts] given by friends and relatives and *anvādheyaka* gifts given by [the husband's] relatives are also [known as *strīdhana*].

Mṛcchakaṭikam

Āryā Dhūtā:

iyaṃ ca me ekā mātṛgṛhalabdhā ratnāvalī tiṣṭhati | *etām apyatiśauṇḍīratayā āryaputro na grahīṣyati.*

(*Mṛcchakaṭikam*, prose after verse 3.26)

Here is one of my necklaces that I received from my mother's family. Even this one my husband will not accept because of his pride.

Cārudattam

Brāhmaṇī [Cārudatta's wife]:

> . . . *mama jñātikulād labdhā śatasahasramūlyā muktāvalī* | *tām āryaputraḥ śauṭīratayā pratīcchati* . . .
>
> (*Cārudattam*, prose portion after act 3, verse 15)

> . . . I received from my natal family a necklace that is valued at one hundred thousand. Would my husband accept that because of his pride?

Cārudatta:

> *mayi dravyakṣayakṣīṇe strīdravyeṇa anukampitaḥ* |
> *arthataḥ puruṣo nārī yā nārī sā arthataḥ pumān* | |
>
> (*Cārudattam*, act 3, verse 17)

> My wealth having been wasted away I am at the mercy of my wife's wealth [being pitied by the wealth of my wife]. In reality then the man has [I have] become the wife and she [has become] the man.

(8) On the purity of women

Baudhāyana Dharmasūtra

> *striyaḥ pavitram atulaṃ naitā duṣyanti karhicit* |
> *māsi māsi rajo hy āsāṃ duritāny apakarṣati* | |
> *somaḥ śaucaṃ dadau tāsāṃ gandharvaḥ śikṣitāṃ giram* |
> *agniś ca sarvabhakṣatvaṃ tasmān niṣkalmaṣā striyaḥ* | |
>
> (*Bau.Dh.Sū.*, 2.4.4–5)

> Women's purity is incomparable. They never become defiled for every month their menstrual blood washes away their [sins].
>
> Soma gave them purity, Gandharva cultivated speech, and Agni the ability to eat anything [they please], whereby women remain untainted.

Vasiṣṭha Dharmasūtra

striyaḥ pavitram atulaṃ naitā duṣyanti karhicit ǀ
māsi māsi rajo hy āsāṃ duṣkṛtāny apakarṣati ǀ ǀ

(*Va.Dha.Sū.*, 5.5; 28.4)

Women's purity is incomparable. They never become defiled for every month their menstrual blood washes away their [sins].

Strīdharmapaddhati

atha rajasvalādharmāḥ ǀ ǀ *tatra Vasiṣṭhaḥ* ǀ ǀ *trirātraṃ rajasvalā rajasvalā aśucucir bhavati* ǀ ǀ

(*Strī.Dh.Pa.*, 32v.8–9, Leslie 1995 [1989], p. 283)

Now, rules about the menstruating woman. Here Vasiṣṭha [says], a menstruating woman remains impure for three nights.

Jñānārnavatantra

dharmādharmaparijñānāt sakale 'pi pavitratā ǀ
vinmūtram strīrajo vāpi nakhāsthi sakalaṃ priye ǀ ǀ

(*Jñānārnavatantra*, 22.26)

One who has the knowledge of *dharma* and *adharma*, to him feces, urine, menstruation, nails and bones, everything is pure.

strīrajaḥ parameśāni dehas tenaiva jāyate ǀ
kathaṃ tam dūṣaṇaṃ yena prāpyate paramapadam ǀ ǀ

(*Jñānārnavatantra*, 22.31)

A body is created from the menstrual blood. Why should we blame that [the body created from the blood] through which one can reach liberation?

(9) On remarriage

Baudhāyana Dharmasūtra

nisṛṣṭāyām hute vāpi yasyai bhartā mṛyeta saḥ ǀ
sā ced akṣatayoniḥ syād gatapratyāgata satī ǀ
paunarbhavena vidhinā punaḥ samskāram arhati ǀ ǀ

(*Bau.Dh.Sū.*, 4.1.16)

If a girl whose husband dies after she has been given away or promised [in nuptial offering], remains a virgin when she returns [home], she can again be married following the rites of *paunarbhava* [i.e., second marriage].

balāccet prahṛtā kanyā mantrair yadi na saṃskṛtā |
. . . *yathā kanyā tathaiva sā* | |

(*Bau.Dh.Sū.*, 4.1.15)

A forcibly abducted virgin, but not wedded, remains a virgin.

Vasiṣṭha Dharmasūtra

yā vā klīvaṃ patitam unmattam vā bhartāram utsṛjya anyaṃ patiṃ vindate mṛte vā sā punarbhūr bhavati | |

(*Va.Dh.Sū.*, 17.20)

Or, she is a remarried woman who marries another husband, leaving her impotent or outcaste or insane or dead husband.

Manusmṛti

nānyotpannā prajā astīha na cānyasya parigrahe |
na dvitīyaś ca sādhvināṃ kvacid bhartopadiśyate | |

(*Manusmmṛti*, 5.160)

No (legal) progeny are begotten here by another man or in another man's wife; nor is a second husband ever prescribed for virtuous women.

(Doniger and Smith 1991, 5.162, p. 116)

Arthaśāstra

nīcatvam paradeśaṃ vā prasthito rājakilbiṣī |
prāṇābhihantā patitas tyājyaḥ klīve api vā patiḥ | |

(*Arthaśāstra*, 3.2.48)

If a husband is of bad character or is long gone abroad, or has become a traitor to his king or likely to endanger the life of his wife, or has fallen from his caste or has lost virility, he may be abandoned by his wife.

(Shamasastry 1967, p. 177)

punarbhūtāyāḥ paunarbhavaḥ

(*Arthaśāstra*, 3.7.12)

Son of a remarried woman is known as *paunarbhava*.

Yājñavalkyasmṛti

akṣatā ca kṣatā caiva punarbhū: . . .

(*Yājñavalkyasmṛti*, 1.67)

Remarried women can be of two kinds, one untouched and the other touched [by her previous husband].

Parāśarasmṛti

naṣṭe mṛte pravrajite klīve ca patite patau |
pañcasv āpatsu nārīṇāṃ patir anyo vidhīyate | |

(*Parāśarasmṛti*, 4.30)

In case of the disappearance or death or renunciation or impotence or lost caste-status of her husband: in these five predicaments, a woman is allowed to take another husband.

Nāradasmṛti

punarbhūs trividhā . . .
kanyaiva akṣatayonir yā pāṇigrahaṇadūṣitā |
punarbhūḥ prathamā proktā punaḥ saṃskāram arhati | |

(*Nāradasmṛti*, 12.45; 12.46)

Remarried women can be of three kinds. . . . A daughter who is a virgin but tainted by having been given away in marriage is known as the first type of remarried woman. [She] needs to go through [marriage] rituals again.

naṣṭe mṛte pravrajite klīve ca patite patau |
pañcasu āpatsu nārīṇāṃ patir anyo vidhīyate | |

(*Nāradasmṛti*, 12.97)

In case of the disappearance or death or renunciation or impotence or lost caste-status of her husband: in these five predicaments, a woman is allowed to take another husband.

Garuḍapurāṇa

naṣṭe mṛte pravrajite klīve ca patite patau |
pañcasu āpatsu nārīṇāṃ patir anyo vidhīyate | |
(*Garuḍapurāṇa*, 107.8.29–30)

In case of the disappearance or death or renunciation or impotence or lost caste-status of her husband: in these five predicaments, a woman is allowed to take another husband.

(10) Reverence for women

Manusmṛti

yatra nāryas tu pūjyante ramante tatra devatāḥ |
yatraitās tu na pūjyante sarvās tatrāphalāḥ kriyāḥ | |
(*Manusmṛti*, 3.56)

Where women are respected, the deities rejoice there, but where they are not respected, all rituals are fruitless.

[Other verses on the same theme from *Manusmṛti* are cited in section 1 of this chapter.]

The *Mahābhārata*

mṛdutvaṃ ca tanutvaṃ ca viklavatvaṃ tathaiva ca |
strīguṇā ṛṣibhiḥ proktā dharmatattvārthadarśibhiḥ | |
(*Mbh, Anuśāsanaparva*, 12.13)

The sages, who discuss the state of *dharma*, say that gentleness, delicacy and timidity are the [proper] attributes of a woman.

pūjanīyā mahābhāgāḥ pūṇyāś ca gṛhadīptayaḥ |
striyaḥ śriyo gṛhasyoktās tasmād rakṣyā viśeṣataḥ | |
(*Mbh, Udyagaparva*, 38.11)

They are to be worshipped, they are pure, sacred and they are the lights of [our] homes. Women are the beauty of our homes. Therefore they are to be protected.

Māhānirvāṇatantra

tava svarūpā ramaṇī jagati ācchannavigrahā |
mohād bhartuścitārohād bhaven narakagāminī | |
(*Māhānirvāṇatantra*, 10.80)

Every woman, O Goddess, is your very form, your body concealed within the universe, and so, if in her delusion a woman should mount her husband's pyre, she would go to hell.

Kulārṇavatantraṃ

yā kācid aṅganā loke sā mātṛkulasambhavā ǀ

(*Kulārṇavatantra* 11.64)

Every woman is born into the family of the Great Mother.

Śaktisaṅgamatantra

nārī trailokyajananī nārī trailokyarūpiṇī ǀ
nārī tribhuvanadhārā nārī dehasvarūpiṇī ǀ ǀ

(*Śaktisaṅgamatantra*, 2.13.43)

Woman is the creator of the universe; the universe is her form.
Woman is the foundation of the world; woman is the form.

na nārīsadṛśaṃ mantraṃ na nārīsadṛśaṃ tapaḥ ǀ
na nārīsadṛśaṃ vittaṃ na bhūtaṃ na bhaviṣyati ǀ ǀ

(*Śaktisaṅgamatantra*, 2.13.49)

There are neither any sacred formula nor any austerity comparable to [the value of] a woman.

There are not, nor has there been, nor will there be any riches more valuable than a woman.

(11) Respect for the mother

The *Mahābhārata*

mātāpitroḥ prajāyante putrāḥ sādhāraṇāḥ kave ǀ
teṣāṃ pitā yathā svāmī tathā mātā na saṁśayaḥ ǀ ǀ

(*Mbh*, *Ādiparva*, 99.28)

Sons are born with equal portions of their mothers' and fathers' selves; hence just as the father is the master of his sons so is the mother. There is no doubt about this.

Yājñavalkyasmṛti

ekadeśam upādhyāyaḥ ṛtvig yajñakṛd ucyate ǀ
ete mānyā yathā pūrvam ebhyo mātā garīyasī ǀ ǀ

(*Yājñavalkyasmṛti*, 1.35)

The brahmin who teaches *ekadeśa mantra* from the Veda is the *upādhyāyaḥ* and the *ṛtvik* helps to perform *yajña*. The mother is to be revered more in comparison to both of them.

(12) On women performing *yajña* and their knowledge of *dharma*

Gobhila Gṛhyasūtra

kāmaṃ gṛhye agnau patnī juhuyāt sāyaṃ prātar homau
gṛhāḥ patnī gṛhya eṣo agnir bhavatīti ।

(*Gobhila Gṛhyasūtra*, 1.3.15)

The wife is the *gṛhā* or home and the fire is called *gṛhyāgni* or fire at home. That is why the wife can perform both day and evening sacrifices, if she wishes.

Women's initiation:

prāvṛtāṃ yajñopavītinīm abhyudānayan japet somo adadat gandharvāya . . . ।

(*Gobhila Gṛhyasūtra*, 2.1.19)

[Then] the girl, covered [by a cloth] and wearing sacred thread is brought forward to be given away with [a *mantra*], '*somo adadat gandharvāya*' . . .

On performing samskāra for a girl child:

ubhābhyāṃ pāṇibhyāṃ mūrdhānaṃ parigṛhya japet tryāyuṣaṃ jamadagner iti । *etayaiva āvṛtā striyās tūṣṇīṃ mantreṇa tu homaḥ* । ।

(*Gobhila Gṛhyasūtra*, 2.9.21–4)

Holding the head [of the son] with both hands, '*tryāyuṣam jamadagne*' [*mantra*] should be uttered. A daughter's [*cūḍākaraṇa*] should be done the same way but silently. But the *mantra* should be uttered during the fire sacrifice.

The *Matsyapurāṇa*

This text holds a different view:

strījātis tu prakṛtyaiva kṛpaṇā dainyabhāṣiṇī ।
śāstrālocansāmarthyām ujjhitaṃ . . .

Women are by nature meek and cannot express themselves. They are unable to discuss *śāstra* . . .

(*Matsyapurāṇa*, 154.156)

The *Mahābhārata*

[Satyavatī's authority: after Vicitravīrya's death Bhīṣma is guided by Satyavatī's advice:]

pretakāryāṇi sarvāṇi tasya samyag akārayat ।
rājño vicitravīryasya satyavatyā mate sthitaḥ ।
ṛtvigbhiḥ sahito bhīṣmaḥ sarvaiś ca kurupuṅgavaiḥ । ।

(*Mbh*, ed. Bhattacharya 1931,
Ādiparva, 96.59)

Following Satyavatī's advice, Bhīṣma performed all of King Vicitravīrya's funerary rites, together with the priests and the entire kuru clan.

vettha dharmaṃ satyavati paraṃ cāparam eva ca ।
yathā ca tava dharmajñe dharme praṇihitā matiḥ । ।

(*Mbh*, ed. Bhattacharya 1931,
Ādiparva, 99.36)

[Mother] Satyavatī, you know the *dharma* of both this world and the next. Your intellect is always immersed in *dharma*.

[Ambā, the daughter of Kāśīrāja, took a vow to kill Bhīṣma who had deprived her of *patidharma* (she was unable to get married). But Bhīṣma was invincible. So she concentrated on her *tapasyā*:]

sāhaṃ bhīṣmavināśāya tapas tapsye sudārūṇam ।
. . .
nirākṛtāsmi bhīṣmeṇa bhraṃśitā patidharmataḥ ।
. . .
vadhārthaṃ tasya dīkṣā me na lokārthaṃ tapodhanāḥ ।
nihatya bhīṣmaṃ gaccheyaṃ śāntim ity eva niścayaḥ । ।

(*Mbh, Udyogaparva*, 187.31; 188.2–3)

I am practising austere meditation to destroy Bhīṣma. I have been deprived of *patidharma* by Bhīṣma. My religious observation is for killing Bhīṣma, not for worldly gain. It is certain that on killing Bhīṣma I shall find peace.

tām devo darśayāmāsa śūlapāṇir umāpatiḥ |
. . .
vadhiṣyasi raṇe bhīṣmaṃ puruṣatvaṃ ca lapsyase |
smariṣyasi ca tat sarvaṃ deham anyam gatā satī | |

(*Mbh, Udyogaparva*, 188.7; 188.12)

God Śūlapāṇi Umāpati revealed himself to her [Ambā]. [He said,] you will kill Bhīṣma in battle and you will also gain manhood. You will remember everything even though you will have a different body.

[Gāndhārī was respected for her adherence to *dharma*:]

kathaṃ ca sadṛśīṃ bhāryāṃ gāndhārīṃ dharmacāriṇim |

(*Mbh, Ādiparva*, 61.98)

Where is a virtuous wife comparable to Gāndhārī?

gāndhāryā dharmaśīlatām . . .

(*Mbh, Ādiparva*, 110)

Gāndharī's adherence to *dharma* . . .

[Kuntī's advice to Yudhiṣṭhira as a *kṣatriya* woman, which she imparts through Kṛṣṇa:]

yudhvasva rājadharmeṇa mā nimajjīḥ pitāmahān |
mā gamaḥ kṣīṇapuṇyatvaṃ sānujaḥ pāpikāṃ gatim | |

(*Mbh, Udyogaparva*, 130.32)

Fight, follow a king's duty, do not drown your ancestors [in shame]! Do not proceed towards lost merit with your brothers by travelling the evil way.

svabāhuvalamāśritya yo abhyujjīvati mānavaḥ |
sa loke labhate kīrtiṃ paratra ca śubhāṃ gatim | |

(*Mbh, Udyogaparva*, 131.42)

A man who preserves life on the strength of his own arms, gains fame in this world and an auspicious journey hereafter.

The *Rāmāyaṇa*

Kausalyā:

kausalyāpi tadā devī rātrīṃ sthitvā samāhitā |
prabhāte cākarot pūjām viṣṇoh putrahitaiṣiṇī | |

(*Rām, Ayodhyākāṇḍa*, 20.14)

Kausalyā, then, having practised austerities through the night, performed *Viṣṇupūjā* in the morning.

Śabarī:

tau puṣkariṇyāḥ pampāyās tīram āsādya paścimam |
apaśyatāṃ tatas tatra śabaryā ramyam āśramam | |

(*Rām, Araṇyakāṇḍa*, 74.4)

The two [Rāma and Lakṣmaṇa] went towards the west bank of Lake Pampā. There they saw the pleasant *āśrama* of Śabarī.

tām uvāca tato Rāmaḥ śramaṇīm dharmasaṃsthitām | |
kaccitte nirjitā vighnāḥ kaccitte vardhate tapaḥ |

(*Rām, Araṇyakāṇḍa*, 74.7–8)

Rāma addressed the female religious mendicant [Śabarī, saying], Have you overcome the obstacles to austerities? Are your religious rites prospering?

(13) On *pātivrātya* or devotion to the husband

Manusmṛti

nāsti strīṇāṃ pṛthag yajño na vrataṃ nāpy upoṣitam |
patiṃ śuśruṣate yena tena svarge mahīyate | |

(*Manusmmṛti*, 5.153)

Women by themselves cannot perform a *yajña* or undertake a vow or a fast. A wife who serves her husband is exalted in heaven.

pāṇigrāhasya sādhvī strī jīvato vā mṛtasya vā |
patilokam abhīpsantī nācared kiñcid apriyam | |

(*Manusmmṛti*, 5.154)

A virtuous wife should never do anything displeasing to the husband who took her hand in marriage, when he is alive or dead, if she longs for her husband's world (after death).

(Doniger and Smith 1991, 5.156, p. 115)

Yājñavalkyasmṛti

strībhir bhartṛvacaḥ kāryam eṣa dharmaḥ paraḥ striyāḥ ।

(*Yājñavalkyasmṛti*, 1.77)

A wife should always listen to her husband. This is the best *dharma* of a wife.

Strīdharmapaddhati

yā strī śuśruṣaṇād bhartuḥ karmaṇā manasā girā ।
taddhitā samavāpnoti tatsālokyam yato dvijaḥ ।।

Since, O twice-born men, a woman who is of benefit to her husband by serving him in thought, word and deed, will come to dwell in the same heaven as he does.

(*Strī.Dh.Pa.*, 22r.3–4, Leslie 1995 [1989], pp. 257–8)

mātaram pitaram vāpi māsmān smara kadācana ।
patireva striy[ā] bandhuḥ patireva striy[ā] dhanam ।
patir eva striy[ā] dharmaḥ patir eva mahat tapaḥ ।

[She should] forget all about us (i.e., her own family), even her mother and father. For the husband alone is a woman's family; the husband alone is a woman's wealth; the husband alone is a woman's religious duty, and her chief austerity.

(*Strī.Dh.Pa.*, 32r.1–2, Leslie 1995 [1989], p. 281)

devavat satataṃ sādhvī bhartāraṃ pratipaśyati ।
patir hi devo nārīṇāṃ patir bandhu patir gatiḥ ।
patyā samā gatir nāsti daivatam vā yathā patiḥ ।।

The good woman always regards her husband as a god . . . For the husband is god for women; the husband is family; the husband is the goal. There is no goal, no deity like the husband.

(*Strī.Dh.Pa.*, 32r.5–6, Leslie 1995 [1989], p. 282)

(14) Women's primary function

Manusmṛti

prajanārthaṃ striyaḥ sṛṣṭāḥ santānārthaṃ ca mānvāḥ |
tasmāt sādhāraṇo dharmaḥ śrutau patnyā sahoditaḥ | |

(*Manusmṛti*, 9.96)

Women were created to bear children, and men to carry on the line; that is why the revealed canon prescribes a joint duty (for a man) together with his wife.

(Doniger and Smith 1991, p. 209)

Arthaśāstra

putrārthā hi striyaḥ

(*Arthaśāstra*, 3.2.42)

Women are [created] to bring forth sons.

Nāradasmṛti

apatyārthaṃ striyaḥ sṛṣṭāḥ . . .

(*Nāradasmṛti*, 12.19)

Women are created for propagation . . .

striyaḥ putravatīm vandyām . . .

(*Nāradasmṛti*, 12.83)

[A man should approach] a woman who has produced sons, who is revered . . .

(15) On sexual morality

Nāradasmṛti

svairiṇy abrāhmaṇī veśyā dāsī niṣkāsinī ca yā |
gamyāḥ syur anulomyena strīyo na pratilomataḥ | |

(*Nāradasmṛti*, 12.78)

A wanton woman, a non-Brahmin, a prostitute, a servant [*dāsī*], or one who is not constrained by her master [*niṣkāsiṇī*] can be approached if she is of the lower caste but not if she is of the higher caste.

(16) A woman's importance

The *Matsyapurāṇa*

striyā virahitā sṛṣṭir jantūnāṃ nopapadyate | |

(*Matsyapurāṇa*, 154.154–5)

No progeny can be born without a woman.

(17) On the importance of one's wife

The *Mahābhārata*

ardhaṃ bhāryā manuṣyasya bhāryā śreṣṭhatamaḥ sakhā |
bhāryā mūlam trivargasya bhāryā mitraṃ mariṣyataḥ | |

(*Mbh, Ādiparva*, 68.40)

A wife is half of a man, a wife is his best friend, and a wife is the base for fulfilling [his] *trivargas* [*dharma, artha* and *kāma*].

nāsti bhāryāsamo bandhur nāsti bhāryāsamo gatiḥ |
nāsti bhāryāsamo loke sahāyo dharmasādhanaḥ | |

(*Mbh, Śāntiparva*, 142.10)

There is no other friend equal to [one's] wife, nor is there [anyone else] equal to her in [showing the ultimate path]. In this world, there is no one else comparable to [one's wife, for] helping in religious rites.

yasya bhāryā gṛhe nāsti sādhvī ca priyavādinī |
araṇyaṃ tena gantavyaṃ yathā araṇyaṃ tathā gṛham | |

(*Mbh, Śāntiparva*, 142.17)

If one does not have a virtuous and pleasant spoken wife at home, he should go to the forest. [For him] forest and home are alike.

(18) Custom and scriptural injunction

Gautama Dharmasūtra

anājñāte daśāvaraiḥ śiṣṭair ūhavadbhir alubdhaiḥ praśastaṃ kāryam |

(*Gau.Dh.Sū.*, 28.48)

In matters that are unclear, one should follow what is endorsed by a minimum of ten persons who are cultured, skilled in reasoning, and free from greed.

(Olivelle 2000, p. 189)

Nāradasmṛti

> *dharmaśāstravirodhe tu yuktiyukto vidhiḥ smṛtaḥ* |
> *vyavahāro hi valavān dharmas tena avahīyate* | |
>
> (*Nāradasmṛti*, 1.40)
>
> When *dharma* and *śāstra* clash, a logical discussion is appropriate. [In such cases], custom prevails [lit: is more powerful] and dharma [here: *śāstra*] is overruled.

Notes

1 Two representative works are Leslie 1992 and Patton 2002. Additional works are included in the bibliography.

2 *svabhāva eṣa nārīṇāṃ narānām iha duṣaṇam.*

(*Manusmṛti*, 2.213.1)

To corrupt men in the world is women's essential nature.

3 On *pātivrātya*, see Leslie 1995 [1989], pp. 257–8, and Leslie 1992, pp. 78, 185, 187, 189.

4 Keith 1920, p. 300.

5 Keith 1914, p. 211.

6 Examples of a number of educated women and their views appear in section 2 of this chapter.

7 The Sanskrit originals of these and other relevant verses from Manu are given in section 2 of this chapter, with translations.

8 The original source is cited in section 2 of this chapter.

9 For a detailed discussion, see Leslie 1995 [1989].

10 For instance, *Pañcatantra* refers to women as the most impure, *aśaucam*, in *Mitrabheda*, 207. See Leslie 1995 [1989], pp. 283–8 for a detailed discussion of this issue.

11 For a detailed discussion, see Sen 1981, pp. 217–37.

12 In *Abhijnnāśakuntalam*, Śakuntalā asserts her dignity when being publicly refused by Duṣyanta in court, she says, 'Evil man! You see everything distorted by your own ignoble heart.'(Act V, prose portion after verse 22). In *Mālavikāgnimitram*, after a dance competition the queen shows her displeasure at the King's action and says 'If my noble lord were to show as much cleverness in arranging affairs of state, we would all prosper' (Act 1, prose passage after verse 19).

13 Jamison in Patton 2002, pp. 69–83.

14 See Krishna Datta, in Bose 2000, pp. 11–14.

15 Medhātithi's commentary on *Manusmṛti*, 5.155.

16 For a detailed discussion, see Datta, in Bose 2000, pp. 7–20.

17 References to the *Mahābhārata* are to the Bhandarkar Oriental Research Institute, Poona edition of 1933–40, unless otherwise stated.

4 Women poets of Hinduism

Mīrābāi

In a philosophical world-view and a social system that allows women little self-determination, one instrument of liberation is that of the poetic imagination. In this chapter we will see how women find in poetry their individual voice unconstrained by social expectations, which they often question or even repudiate. Whether the poets were writing of their spiritual quest or of their experience of the secular world or, occasionally, of that world's skewed view of women, they struggled for liberation by means of their act of self-construction through language.

The language arts of India comprised, till modern times, one of the few domains in which women could speak in their own voices when they could not on common public platforms. What was the ideal that allowed them to do so? In our examination of Hindu goddesses in Chapter 2, we noted how such figures – idealized representations of energy – have been translated through time into role models for Hindu women, and how in the process the ideals for women have shifted in focus from authority to conformity. But the discussion there also marked out one goddess who does not, for all her gentleness, fall into a dependency role. This is Sarasvatī, the goddess of learning and the arts, whose example hardly prepares women for the domestic roles of wife or mother enjoined upon women in Hindu society. On the contrary, she may be said to give women their voice because she validates speech, women's as much as men's. Even then it has not been easy for women in traditional Hindu society to pursue the arts of language for any but the most commonplace jobs of life, for speech can be liberating and always holds the potential for self-assertion and resistance. Such freedom could well be viewed with suspicion. It is not surprising, then, that until the adoption of liberal educational policies in India from the nineteenth century, women who sought learning were often considered neglectful of their womanly responsibility of looking after their families.[1] But that is just why seeking Sarasvatī's blessings might be regarded by women as a way to independence, if not always in practical life, at least in imagination's domain. Whether this has ever been the actual reasoning behind women's pursuit of learning and the arts cannot be determined, but it is historically evident that poetry has been a particularly effective medium for women in their struggle to voice their individual identities.

It is important to identify what ideological precedents and social routes are available for women if they are to search for alternatives to their conventional roles. Other than Sarasvatī, the other locus of independence is the even more commanding presence among Hindu divinities, one who cannot be forced into any domestic role, the terrible yet loving goddess Kālī. Even though she is associated with Śiva, she conducts herself as no wife or homemaker one may imagine! Her relationship with Śiva is direct, as an equal, and never conditional upon submission to any prescribed role. This may explain why some women have sought her aid in discovering the ecstasy of spiritual life without the mediation of institutions of worship but in the liberating idiom of poetry. Among the women poets we shall consider in this chapter there are three – Kāraikkāl Āmmāiār, Lāllā Yogeśvarī and Mahādevī Ākkā – who, as devotees of Śiva, emulated Kālī in formulating and expressing their love for Lord Śiva in their writings. Devotion to Kālī, though, is not the only inspiration for Hindu women poets; two major poets studied in this chapter, Āṇṭāl and Mīrābāi, reach the greatest height of ecstasy in their surrender to Kṛṣṇa, whereby they seek their release from their world's expectations. At the same time, the need for spiritual liberation may not be untouched by the recognition of society's tyranny, of which we find striking examples in the works of two poets studied here, Ātukuri Mollā from Andhra and Candrāvatī from Bengal.

The work of women in the realm of poetry is particularly interesting as efforts at claiming selfhood. What this chapter attempts to show is that it was in that realm that in pre-modern times women in Hindu society found an opportunity for self-assertion, and that despite its patrifocal ethic and power structure, their world included a platform for women to achieve an autonomous selfhood through the arts in general and poetry in particular as an art uniting intellect, heart, eye and hand. In poetry women's work took many different routes. While their creativity flowed for the most part into spiritual channels, some women, though not very many, also responded to secular and social experience. This variety stands as evidence that the arts have functioned as instruments of release from the constrictions of the social world and provided an effective mode of achieving both spiritual and social autonomy. Parallel evidence comes from the rich heritage of women's creativity in music and the decorative arts such as murals and fabric work, but here I shall focus on women's poetry, using collections of women's writings as well as individual works.[2] Since a comprehensive study of all women poets from every region of India would be a daunting task, we shall limit ourselves to a selection of poems by some of the best known women poets from different linguistic and cultural regions of India who were searching for a higher reality above the immediacy of earthly life.

We must note at this point that these poets were indeed well-known but as far as we can tell, known only within their own geographic and linguistic space. As in other cultures, in the Hindu tradition too, women's voices from pre-modern times – in fact till the nineteenth century – have had scarcely any opportunity of being heard and it was not till the twentieth century that the publication of the works of early women writers was undertaken, and even then only sporadically. In the very long pre-industrial era of Indian civilization, through the greater part of which women had little public presence, they had small chance of being heard except within their immediate social circle. Even within that narrow world, in which women's primary and only meaningful identity was deemed to be that of a caregiver, poetic aspirations would have faced insurmountable prejudice. Thus there can be no estimate of how many women might have given literary expression to their thoughts and feelings, or from what time precisely. We do know that many women held positions of honour in early India, that there were women philosophers, and that some were regarded as *brahmavādinīs*, of whom twenty-seven are known to us by name and historical references to their work.[3] Whether any of them wrote poetry is impossible even to guess.

SECTION 1: IN LOVE WITH GOD: THE MYSTICAL EXPERIENCE

In the history of literature from pre-modern India, women are largely represented in the domain of religious poetry. For women who devoted themselves to the quest for god, poetry was a mode of cutting through the illusions of the material world in order to reach for spiritual reality. Leaving the world behind, women ascetics attempted to free themselves from the dictates of social conventions and assert an independent subjectivity – paradoxically – through their surrender to a personal god. Their medium for giving shape to the powerful emotions this quest generated was the poetry of personal experience.

The first recorded poetry in India definitively attributed to women was by Buddhist nuns, or *theris*, of the sixth century B.C.E and was known as *Therigāthās*, that is, songs of *theris*. They were first collected, translated into English and published in 1909 by C. A. F. Rhys-Davids, later expanded with contributions from K. R. Norman.[4] The emphasis common to these very short poems is the elation of escaping an oppressive social world by embracing religion. These poems do not explore or expound the philosophical ideas of Buddhism but speak of the freedom that the authors have found in their religious life, and the chance they now have of achieving spiritual emancipation. The power of these short statements comes from this dual sense of release. What animates these poems is the sense of freedom, and freedom is understood both as a spiritual and a social experience, as these examples show:

Muttā:

> O free, indeed! O gloriously free
> Am I in freedom from three crooked things:
> From quern, from mortar, from my crookback'd lord.
> Ay, but I'm freed from rebirth and from death,
> And all that dragged back is hurled away.
> (Rhys Davids and Norman, tr. 1989, p. 11, verse 11)

Sumanā:

> Hast thou not seen sorrow and ill in all
> The springs of life? Come thou not back to birth!
> Cast out the passionate desire again to Be
> So shall thou go thy ways calm and serene!
> (Rhys Davids and Norman, tr. 1989, p. 14, verse 14)

In these terse statements we see an utter disenchantment with worldly life, even physical life itself ('to Be'), against which a life of renunciation shines as a beacon of serenity. The impulse we encounter here for turning away from the material to the spiritual world is characteristic of women's poetry also in the Hindu tradition but in that tradition it finds much greater elaboration of thought and feeling and in more sophisticated literary form.

These first known poetic utterances in the religious idiom attributable to women in India are followed by more emphatic feminine voices from about the fifth century C.E. that explore spirituality in strikingly original ways. But early as they were, these female authors of Hindu religious poetry were in fact preceded by even earlier women poets from South India, except that the South Indian poets wrote in the secular mode, of which we shall speak later. Of the women writing in the religious vein whose writings have survived, we shall focus on four in particular, Āṇṭāl, Ākkā Mahādevī, Lāllā Yogeśvarī and Mirābāi, examining their poems in the original languages followed by English translations, but we shall also look at others in passing, though only in translation.* The common thread that runs through these poems is the determination with which the authors launched their spiritual journey right from their childhood, pursuing their love for god despite all the obstacles that conventional social regulations and expectations could throw up against them.

The other common element is an originality of vision that takes the poets outside the boundaries of self-effacing speech expected of women, as illustrated by the writings of one of the earliest women poets, Kāraikkāl Āmmāiār, who lived sometime between the fifth and the seventh centuries and wrote in Tamil.[5] Even in her own time she came to be recognized as one of the sixty devotees of Śiva known as the *nāyanmārs*. All her surviving poems articulate her yearning to transcend the barriers of worldly affairs and the limitations of the flesh, including her own beauty, to reach for an unobstructed view of the reality of the Lord divested of ceremony. Her yearning for liberation from this world was so intense that on finding herself estranged from her husband, she pleaded:

> So I pray to Thee that the flesh of my body, which has been sustaining beauty for his sake, may now be removed from my physical frame and I may be granted the form of the ghosts which dance round Thee with devotion.
>
> (S. Pillai, 1955, pp. 18–19)

Rejecting the limited vision of ordinary mortals, she saw beyond mere appearance:

> They who are incapable of understanding His real nature make fun of Him. They see only His fine form besmeared with ashes and bedecked with a garland of bones like a ghost.
>
> (S. Pillai, 1955, p. 21)

Capable as she was of looking beyond the immediate, she saw the beauty of her lord, Śiva, underneath his beggarly exterior. It was her ability to see the reality beneath materiality that prompted her to emulate Kālī in her own appearance both as a rejection of external show and as a gesture of belief in the beauty and grace inherent in the goddess visible to the transcendent imagination.

* Unless otherwise indicated, translations are mine.

Outstanding among early woman poets is Āṇṭāl, a commanding figure both as a poet and as an object of continuing devotion. This *vaiṣṇava* woman from ninth century Tamil Nadu was regarded as one of twelve *ālvārs* or exemplars of Viṣṇu *bhakti* and is now worshipped as a consort of Kṛṣṇa in the Srirangam temple,[6] whose works, it is claimed, predate the *Bhāgavatapurāṇa*, one of the most influential texts of Hinduism.[7] Admiration for her is so great that a distinct hagiography has grown up around her, parts of which have turned her into a mythical personage. One story, for instance, sees her, like Sītā, as an infant found by her adoptive father in the furrows of his field when he was searching for the sacred plant *tulasī*, which of course imparts holiness to her by association. Beginning a life of total devotion to Kṛṣṇa as a very young girl, Āṇṭāl remained unmarried because she considered herself a bride of Kṛṣṇa. In some of her poems she portrays herself as a maiden eager for union with Kṛṣṇa. In others she imagines herself as his bride and recalls in erotic imagery the joy of her mystical union with him. These two related but different types of declarations are organized as two distinct groups of short poems, groups that are aligned as consecutive parts of a total regime of devotion over a two-month period. The first part, called *Tiruppāvai*, represents the earlier phase of her spiritual journey as a trope of the Tamil tradition of the *pāvai* vow observed in the month of Mārkali, which corresponds to the period of mid-December to mid-January. It is undertaken by young girls to ensure a happy marriage, preparing themselves for it by self-purification and inviting their desired one by making idealized clay images and singing songs of invitation and praise. It is easy to see how well this would lend itself to Āṇṭāl's yearning for her Lord, especially as the ritual ends in celebrating the arrival of the beloved – in her case the assertion of a mystical sense of experiencing the Lord's presence. In the poems of Āṇṭāl's *Tiruppāvai* celebration, it is this sense of self-preparation and joy that we encounter, as these examples show:

Mārkālit tiṅkāl mati nirayinta nannālāl |
Nīrāṭap potuvīr potumino, nerilaiyir!
Cīr malkum āipāṭic celvac cirumīrkāl!
Kūr ver koṭuntolilan nantokopan kumāran
Er ārnta kaṇṇi uacotai ilanciṅkam
Kār menic ceṅkan katirmatiyam pol mukattān
Nārāyaṇane namakke parai taruvān;
Pāror pukalap paṭintu-elor empāvāi.

(Sundaram 1987, *Tiruppāvai*, p. 2, verse 1)

The month of Mārkali's full moon is here
This auspicious morning.
O maidens bejeweled!
Come out,
Those who wish to bathe in this water clear.
O sweet maidens
Of blessed cowherd clan!

Nanda's son,
Cruel as a sharp spear,
Young lion,
Child of Yaśodā of loving eyes,
With his dark body and
Visage like the Sun and the Moon,
Rosy-orbed One!
Will fulfill our desire.

Nārāyana himself has offered us his drums,
To sing his praise
And gain the world's applause.

Vaiyattu vālvīrkāl! Nāmum nam pāvaikkuc
Ceyyum kiricaikal keliro; parkaṭalul . . .
(Sundaram 1987, *Tiruppāvai*, p. 4, verse 2, st. 1)

O Worldly people,
Listen to what we do
To observe our *pāvai* vow.

The second group of Āṇṭāl's poems is the *Nācciyār Tirumozhi* set, which imitates a worship vow as does the first part. The celebration it purportedly recreates is a follow-up of the *Tiruppāvai* ritual vow. It takes place in the month of Tai (mid-January to mid-February) immediately after the month of Mārkali, which is dedicated to the *Tiruppāvai Tirumozhi.* Tai is a period of prayer and worship that expresses the devotee's anguish at the uneasy feeling that the Lord, whose presence had been felt at the end of *Tiruppāvai,* is no longer close. As Āṇṭāl recalls the joys of her union with her Lord, she is struck by the pain of separation, and this she understands and expresses in the human idiom of love and physical desire. Speaking as a bride separated from her spouse, she embodies her love in highly sexual imagery that humanizes God and marks the speaker's spiritual approximation of the divine as a concrete experience rather than as an abstraction.

Further examples show how the spiritual and the material meet in Āṇṭāl's imagination:

> *Kāy uṭai nelloṭu karumpu amaittu,*
> *Kaṭṭi arici aval amaittu,*
> *Vai uṭai maraiyavar mantirattāl,*
> *Manmatane! unnai vanaṅkukinren;*
> *Teyam munalantavan tirivikkiraman,*
> *Tirukkaikalāl ennait, tiṇṭum vaṇṇam*
> *Cāy uṭai vayirum en taṭa mulaiyum*
> *Taraṇiyil talaippukal tarakkirriye* |
>
> (Sundaram 1987, *Nācciyar Tirumozhi,* p. 41, hymn 1, verse 7)

> O Manmatha, I invoke you!
> With sugarcane and pressed rice
> Cooked in palm-sugar.
> I worship you
> With sacred hymns in your praise.
>
> Bless me,
> So that Trivikrama,
> Who spanned the world three times,
> May caress with his sacred hands
> My breasts and my waist
> With love,
> Granting me fame on earth
> And glory eternal!

> *Caṅka mā kaṭal kaṭaināṉ tan mukilkāl!*
> *veṅkaṭattuc*
> *Cenkaṇ māl cevaṭik kīl aṭī-vilcci viṇṇappam:*
> *Koṅkai mel kuṅkummattin kulampu aliyap*
> *pukuntu oru nāl*
> *Taṅkumel, en āvi taṅkum enru uraiyire.*
>
> (Sundaram 1987, *Nācciyar Tirumozhi,* p. 104, hymn 8, verse 7)

> O cool clouds
> From the conch-filled ocean
> The lotus-eyed Venkata churned,
> Lay at His feet

My humble plea–
Tell him:
Enter me
Only for a day,
Wipe away the saffron
On my breasts.
I will then live.

A later poet, Mahādevī Ākkā came from twelfth-century Karnataka. A follower of the *Vīraśaiva* sect, she was initiated into Śiva worship at the age of ten by an unknown guru and she took that event as marking the moment of her real birth. She betrothed herself to Śiva and rejected all others even though many human lovers pursued her with urgent suits. She was finally married to Kauśika, a king who had fallen in love with her, but Ākkā never accepted that marriage as real, for, apart from being merely human, the king was a *bhāvī* or an unbeliever and therefore ill-qualified to be a righteous husband. When Kauśika attempted to force her into submission, she left him in disavowal of her marriage as a gesture not only of defiance to his power but also of social norms. So strong was her conviction of being beyond the rule of the human world that she wandered the land naked, with her body covered in nothing but her tresses, walking towards Kalyāṇa, a centre of *Vīraśaiva* saints, where she was not accepted till after she extensively debated noted saints such as Āllāmā. When Āllāmā asked, 'Why take off clothes, as if by that gesture you could peel off illusions? And yet robe yourself in tresses of hair? If so free and pure in heart, why replace a sari with a covering of tresses?'. Ākkā answered, 'Till the fruit is ripe inside, the skin will not fall off.'[8] At the end of this ordeal by disputation, she was accepted in the company of the sages. What this exchange shows is a remarkable mix of Ākkā's courage of conviction, her power of philosophical perception and her command over metaphoric invention.

Her induction into the company of sages gave her the independence from social restrictions she needed, allowing her to wander about in search of Śiva, whom she is thought to have found on Śrīśaila, the Holy Mountain. The poems she composed throughout her quest record her yearning for the Lord in the idiom of traditional love poetry, using the three main forms of love recognized in formal literature. The first, love forbidden, is expressed thus:[9]

Atte māye, māva saṁsāri,
Mūvaru maidunaru huliyanthavaru.

Nālvaru nageveṇṇu kēḷu keḷadi
Aivaru bhāvadiranoyva deivavilla
Āru attigeyara mīralārenu tāye.
Hēḷuvaḍe yeḷu tottira kāhu
Karmavemba gaṇḍana bāya ṭoṇedu
Hādaravanāḍuvenu haranakoḍe
Manavemba sakhiya prasādadinda
Anubhavava kalitenu Śivanoḍane
Kara celuva śrīśaila Cennamallikārjuna
Sajjana gaṇḍana māḍikombe.
(Menezes and Angadi 1973, p. 8, verse 21)

Māyā is my mother-in-law,
The world is my father-in-law.
Three tiger-like younger brothers-in-law,
And four sisters-in-law,
Five elder brothers-in-law,
I have.

Many women watch over me for my husband,
He is no god, my husband!

I shall escape and cuckold him with Hara,
My Lord!

My mind is my friend,
With her help I shall wed my Lord
The beautiful Siva from Sriśaila,
Cenna Mallikārjuna, my groom.

The second form of love poetry, about love in separation, is adopted in the following passage:

Tānu daṇḍu mṇḍalakke hōdahenendaḍe nānu summa nihenallade
Tānenna kaiyoḷagiddu, tānenna manadoḷagiddu
Ennakoḍa nuḍiyadiddarānu entu sairisuvenavvā?
Nēhavemba kuṇṭaṇi Cennamallikārjunana nerahadirdaḍe
Nānēve sakhiye?
(Menezes and Angadi 1973, p. 18, verse 60)

If he has to go to the battlefield
I can understand and be quiet.
But when he is here on my palm
And within my heart,

How can I bear it,
If he does not speak to me?
If the memory of love
Does not make Cenna Mallikārjuna love me,
How will I bear it?

Next comes the third kind of love poetry, about love in union:

Maccu accugavāgi oppida pariya nōḍā!
Eccaḍ e gariōradantirabēku.
Appidaḍ āstigaḷ u nuggu-nusūgabēku.
Beccaḍ e besuge hariyadantirabēku.
Maccu oppittu Cennamallikārjunayyana snēha.

(Menezes and Angadi 1973,
p. 14, verse 43)

Behold love's wonderful ways!
When you shoot your arrow
Take care to plant it well
So that the feather does not show
When you hug a body, bones crack and crumble,
Join but the joint must not show–
How wonderful then is the love of Cenna Mallikārjuna!

Applying the traditional imagery of Indian love poetry to the experience of spiritual longing and consummation, Ākkā metaphorizes the phases of human love as the phases of a mystical approach to the divine, drawing her images from nature, birds and beasts. As in secular love poetry, Ākkā's divine lover is an aesthetic construction whom she addresses as Cennamallikārjuna or the Lord White as Jasmine. By the time she died in her twenties, Ākkā had given voice to the widest imaginable range of the human yearning for the divine in humanly understandable rhetoric in countless poems, of which the small selection below is worth pondering:

Teraṇ iya ḥulu tanna sēhadinda maneyamāḍi
Tanna nolu tannannē sutti sāva teranante
Manabanduda bayāsi bayasi bēvuttiddēnayyā
Aiyyā indu nīnolidu enna manada durāśeya māṇ isi
Nimmatta tōrā Cennamallikārjunā.

(Menezes and Angadi 1973,
p. 68, verse 171)

Like a silkworm that secretes her dwelling,
Wrapping herself tightly
With her body's thread and dies,
I am dying, pining for my heart's desire.
Help me, O Lord, cut all my greed,
Show me the way to you,
Cenna Mallikārjuna!

Kaisiriya danḍava koḷabahudallade
Maisiriya danḍava koḷaluṇṭe?
Uṭṭanta uḍuge – toḍugeyanalla seḷedukoḷabahandallade
Muccimusukirda nirvāṇava seḷdukoḷabahude?
Cennamallikārjuna dēvara beḷaganuṭṭu lajjegeṭṭavaḷige
uḍuge-toḍugeya haṅgēkō maruḷe?

(Menezes and Angadi 1973, p. 62, verse 146)

You can confiscate the riches in hand,
But how can you take away the body's glory?

You can strip off clothes from the body
But how can you take away nothingness
That wraps around the body?

For one who adorns herself
With the morning light of
Lord Cenna Mallikārjuna,
Shedding all shame,
Where is the need for cover and veil?

Yenagēkaiyyā nā prapañcina putthaḷi?
Māyikada malabhāṇḍa; āturada bhavaniḷaya!
Jalakumbhada aḍeyalli vasaruva nelevenegēkaiyyā?
Beraḷu tāḷa haṇṇa hisukidoḍe melaluṇṭe?
Bittella jīva adaroppada tera enage
Enna tappa vappugoḷḷā!
Cennamallikārjuna dēvara dēva nīve aṇṇagaḷirā!

(Menezes and Angadi 1973, p. 60, verse 139)

Why must I be a puppet
Of this world? A cask of illusion?
A worldly mansion peopled by passions,
Leaking at its foundation?
With your finger you may

Feel and squeeze the fig
But can you eat it?
. . .
O Cenna Mallikārjuna, take me
With my faults and all.

Sāvillada sahajange rohillada celuvange
Bhavavillada abhavange, bhayavillada nirbhaya celuvange
Nānolidenayya
Cennamallikārjuna gaṇḍanenage
Mikkina lōkada gaṇḍarenage sambandhavillavayya!
(Menezes and Angadi 1973, p. 16, verse 51)

I love the beautiful One,
The formless One.

He has no death nor decay
The beautiful, the fearless, the dauntless One,
Beyond birth is He . . .

Cenna Mallikārjuna is my Lord –
Take these mortal husbands
And feed them to the fire in the kitchen.

Another *śaiva* poet but one from a later period, a different place and a different philosophical school was the Kashmiri poet Lāllā Yogeśvarī, also called Lāl Ded. At the age of 24, her sufferings at the hands of her husband and in-laws drove her to leave family life and choose the life of a renunciate, into which she was initiated by a Kashmiri *śaivaite* guru. She combined intellectual devotionalism with the esotericism of *tāntric yoga*, and this philosophical orientation led her to employ the technical language of monistic *vedānta* with that of *tāntric* philosophy. Like Mahādevī Ākkā, Lāllā became a mendicant, similarly dispensing with her clothes and attaining *mokṣa* early in the course of her long life. A *nirguṇa bhakta*, that is, the devotee of an abstraction rather than that of a personified divinity, she distinguished herself as a philosopher by seeking union not with a personal deity but with an abstract, unqualified principle, with which she claimed her oneness. Because of this philosophical position her poetry deals more with abstractions than with emotional experience. Her sense of Śiva as an idea rather than a bodily presence invests all her poetry with the excitement of philosophical thought rather than that of personal relationship, as these examples illustrate:[10]

śiv vā keśav jin vā kamluj | |
nāthā nāv dhāriniy yo yo | |
so mi abali kāsītan bhavaruj
so vā so vā so vā so | |

Let Him bear the name of Śiva, or of Keśava, or of the Jina,
or of the Lotus-born Lord – whatever name he bear –
May he take from me, sick woman that I am, the disease of
the world,
Whether He be he, or he, or he, or he.

(Grierson and Barnett 1920, p. 30, verse 2)

par tā pān | | *yamī samoy māno*
hihoy mānon din ta rāt | |
yamī advay man sampanno
tamī diṭṭho suragurunāth | |

He who hath deemed another and himself as the same,
He who hath deemed the day (of joy) and the night (of sorrow)
to be alike,
He whose mind hath become free from duality,
He, and he alone, hath seen the Lord of the Chiefest of gods.

(Grierson and Barnett 1920, p. 27, verse 29)

manas man | | *bhavasaras* | |
choḍhyū kop | | *niris tā nārachyvak* | |
likān | | *lachy* | | *tūlā koṭū* | |
tuli tūlo tā tul nā ak | |

Look upon thy mind alone as the ocean of existence.
If thou restrain it not, but let it loose, from its rage will issue
angry words, like wounds caused by fire.
If you weigh them in the scales of truth, their weight is
naught.

(Grierson and Barnett 1920, p. 45, verse 12)

Nāthā pānā nā parjānā |
Sādhit bādhim eha kudeha | |
Ci bhu cū mi milo nā jānā |
Cū ku bhu ku chyoṁ sandeha | |

Lord, I have not known myself
Or other than myself.
Continually have I mortified this vile body.

That Thou art I, that I am Thou, that these are joined in one
I knew not.
It is doubt to say, 'Who am I?' and 'Who are Thou?'
(Grierson and Barnett 1920, p. 29, verse 5)

Perhaps the best-known of the women poets within the Hindu religious tradition is Mīrābai, the princess from Rajasthan who encountered relentless persecution from her husband for her absolute absorption in the contemplation of Kṛṣṇa. Legend has her married to the crown prince of Mewar, but for her it was a marriage only in name, for she thought of herself as married to Kṛṣṇa, whom she addressed as Giridhārī Nāgara. Mīrā refused to pay obeisance to her mother-in-law and even to the dynastic deity, which drew upon her head endless torment. For instance, her sisters-in-law tried to stop her from meeting *sādhus* as an activity improper to her birth and her married status. When her husband failed to turn her from her allegiance to Giridhārī Nāgara, his idea of honour drove him to try to kill her on two occasions but each time she miraculously escaped death, by Kṛṣṇa's grace, according to legend. Mirā spent most of her adult life in worship and devotion, eventually leaving Mewar and travelling east as a pilgrim to places sanctified by Kṛṣṇa's presence, such as Brajabhūmi, and later back west to Dvārakā. It is not known for certain when and how she died but the numerous legends about her tell how, when she could not stop being forced back to her husband's domain by the pleas of his brahmin priests, she entered Kṛṣṇa's temple and never re-appeared, for she had been taken to his bosom by Kṛṣṇa himself.

Mīrā's poetical works consist of songs addressed to Giridhārī and these songs comprise, with those of Tulasīdās and Sūrdās, almost the entire body of Hindusthani devotional music. Since Mīrā thought of Kṛṣṇa as a *saguṇa* being, an embodied divinity, her imagination endowed him with personal form and character, much of it playful. In her songs she sees herself in a relationship with Kṛṣṇa as a real entity whose presence is always actual, immediate and intimate, a familiar being whom she places in every kind of loving relationship of domesticity, including those of a bride, friend and mother. In place of the passionate fervour of Āṇṭāl or philosophical brilliance of Lāllā, here we have a gentle though all-consuming love that seeks only the submersion of the self in the divine, which she understands as the essence of love. This absorption in love is perhaps the reason why Mīrā's songs continue to move scholars and common people alike, filling them with a promise of God's accessibility, as these examples will show:

sāṁvariyo raṅg rāṁcā rāṇā, sāṁvariyo raṅg rāṁcā |
tāla pakhāvajāṁ mirdaṅg bājāṁ, sādhāṁ āge ṇācāṁ | |
būjhayā māṇe madaṇ bābarī, śyām prītamhāṁ kāṁcāṁ |
bikhro pyālo rāṇāṁ bhejyāṁ ārogyāṁ ṇo jāṁcāṁ |
mīrāṁ re prabhu giradhara nāgara, jaṇama jaṇama sāṁcaṁ | |

(Tiwari 1974, p. 201, verse 48)

I am dyed in love for the Dark One, Rāṇā, dyed in love for the Dark One,
Clapping to the beat of drums, I dance before the sages.
My mother said I was mad to be in love, for Śyām's love is fleeting.
I drank the cup of poison the Rāṇā sent me, asking no questions.

Mīrā's Lord is the handsome Giridhārī whose love holds true through the ages.

ācche mīṭhe cākh cākh ber lāī bhīlṇī |
aisī kahā acārvatī, rūp nahī ek ratī,
nice kul ochī jāt, ati hi kucīlṇī |
jūṭhe phal līnheṁ rām, prem kī pratīt jāṇ,
ūṁc nīc jāne nahī, ras kī rasīlnī |
aisī kahā ved paḍhi, chiṇ meṁ vimāṇ caḍhī,
hari jī sūṁ bāṁdhyo hetu baikuṇṭh me jhulṇī |
dās mīrā rahai soi aisī prīti karai joi,
patit pāvan prabhu gokul ahīrṇī | |

(Sharma 1972, p. 343, verse 185)

The Bhil woman brought the good, sweet plums, tasting each first.
The devout woman said, 'She has not a grain of beauty,
This low-caste, low-born woman in unsightly rags.'
Rāma took the soiled fruits, knowing they were marks of love,
For he knows nor high nor low, only that she has the taste for love.
What Veda has she studied? Yet in a flash she mounted a chariot
Bound for a swing in heaven put up by Hari just for her.
Your servant Mīrā is like all who have such love.
My Lord, Saviour of the fallen, take unto you the cowherd girl of Gokula.

cālāṁ agama vā des, kāl dekhyāṁ ḍarāṁ ।
bharāṁ prem rā hoj, haṁsa kelyāṁ karāṁ ।
sādhā santa ro saṅg, gyāṇ jugtāṁ karāṁ ।
dharāṁ sāṁvaro, dhyān citta ujalo karāṁ ।
sīl ghūṁghrā bāṁdh tos niratā karāṁ ।
sājāṁ sol siṁgār, soṇāro rākhḍāṁ ।
sāṁvaliyā sūṁ prīt, aurāṁ sūṁ ākhḍāṁ ।
(Sharma 1972, p. 350, verse 192)

Let us go to that unreachable land that death fears to see,
To that lake brimming with love, on which swans play,
And the company of sages and saints brings wisdom,
The mind alight as it cleaves to the Dark One,
Wearing ankle bells of pure thought, all dance in contentment
And decked in golden bracelets practice the sixteen arts of delight,
In love with the Dark Lord, turning away from all others.

Even on a first reading of the poems quoted here it is hard not to be persuaded that their authors were not only superb writers but also original thinkers. Their profound spirituality apart, the assertion of their independence from all dictates of society marks them out as revolutionary personalities. And the few poets represented here, who do stand above most other women poets of all time and a great many male poets as well, were by no means rare practitioners of their art. Among women of significant achievement we must count Jānābāi and Bahiṇībāi from Maharashtra, Ātukuri Mollā from Andhra, Gaṅgāsatī and Ratanbāi from Gujrat, Rāmi and Candrāvatī from Bengal, and many more. In their and other women's poetry we find an ever-widening variety of experience, perception and poetic strategy as we travel down the ages, often coloured by their acknowledgment of the restraints upon women's lives or even their pain, as in the works of Jānābāi (1298–1350) and Bahiṇībāi (1628–1700). Jānābāi comforts herself by recalling the common state of the world:

Let me not be sad because I am born a woman
In the world; many saints suffer in this way
(Tharu and Lalitha 1991, p. 82)

Bahiṇībāi reacts to strictures on women sharply:

Veda hāṁkā detī purāṇe garjatī ।
striyecyā saṅgatīṁ hita nohe । ।

mīṁ to sahaja striyecācī deha |
paramārthācī soya ātāṁ kaiṁcī | |
mūrkhtva mamatā mohana māyika |
saṅgacī ghātaka striyecā to | |
bahiṇī mhṇe aisā strīdeha ghātakī |
paramārtha yā lokīṁ kaibīm sādhe | |

(Abbott 1929, p. 213, *Abhaṅga*, 63)

(1) The Vedas cry aloud, the Purāṇas shout that no good comes of a woman. (2) Now I in the natural way have a woman's body. What means then have I to acquire the supreme spiritual riches [*paramārtha*]? (3) The characteristics (of a woman) are foolishness, selfishness, seductiveness, ad deception. All connection with a woman is disastrous. (Such is their opinion.) (4) Says Bahiṇī, 'If a woman's body brings disaster, what chance is there for her to acquire in this life the supreme spiritual riches?'.

(Abbott 1929, p. 39, *Abhaṅga*, 63)

But despite her protest against the denigration of women, she accepts her traditional role as a wife and declares her devotion to her husband:

citta heṁ bhratārāviṇ jarī jāye |
tarī vās hoy narakīṁ āmhāṁ | |
bhratāradarśanāviṇ jāy dīsa |
tarī tecī rāsa pātakāñcī | |
bahiṇī mhṇe maja ājñācī pramāṇa |
brahma sanātana svāmī mājhā | |

(Abbott 1929, p. 204, *Abhaṅga*, 37)

(5) If my heart wanders from my husband, then my abode will be hell. (6) If a day should pass without seeing my husband, that in itself will be a great heap of sins. (7) Says Bahiṇī, 'His commands are my law. My Svāmi is himself the Eternal Brahma.'

(Abbott 1929, p. 26, *Abhaṅga*, 37)

SECTION 2: SPEAKING OF THE WORLD: THE VOICE OF EXPERIENCE

The samples given above of the works of Jānābāi and Bahiṇībāi present direct responses to the burden women seem born to bear. Women like them, who wrote in the religious strain, were clearly not unaware of the heavy hand of society, though they may not have cared what society thought, having secured their personal freedom by turning society's strictures irrelevant. But were we to shift some of these poems from a religious to a secular framework, they might well be taken to articulate resistance to the gender typology that characterizes a strong trend of Hindu thought. This is not to claim that these poems should be taken as gestures of conscious defiance; that they are, however, keenly aware of a social system tilted against women is hardly debatable.

Bridging the religious and the secular stands Ātukuri Mollā, an early sixteenth-century woman of the *lingāyat* potter caste born to parents who were devotees of Śrīkaṇṭha Malleśvara. Mollā – the name stands for jasmine – accepted a challenge from the brahmins and composed in five days a Telugu version of the *Rāmāyaṇa* in 138 stanzas in six chapters.[11] Secure in her devotion, she asserts her faith both in her lord and her poetic ability in these lines:

> I have no credentials in the field of phonetics,
> I can't spout declensions and root derivations,
> I'm unschooled in tropes, or rhythms; the artifice
> of prosody is not my thing either.
>
> I lack the formal training in writing poetry
> and composing long narratives,
> I haven't scanned handbooks of style
> or familiarized with lexicons of grammar.
>
> But only by the grace of the renowned Lord,
> Shri Kantha Mallesha, somehow I've been blessed–
> I find I am able to write these verses.
>
> (Jackson 2005, p. 83)

In these lines Mollā declares her faith at the same time as she claims her place in the community of letters. When she legitimates herself by invoking 'the renowned Lord', she is not expressing the same kind of spiritual passion as we have found in the poetry of Āntāl or Mīrā but adopting the rhetoric of religion to set up her personal authority against the strictures of her would-be social masters. The poetic exchange here is not so much between deity and devotee as between the author and her material world.

Responding to the material world and the conditions it imposes on the writer is a cultural phenomenon of long heritage within Hindu culture. Centuries before Mollā we find a powerful tradition of secular poetry in the vibrant *cankam* culture of South India extending from about 100 B.C.E. to 300 C.E. This is the period from which has come the earliest known poetry by Hindu women. The poems are secular and fall into two thematic groups, one relating to women's responses to the warrior culture they lived in, the other to private emotional experience. The figure that dominates both types of poetry is a woman called Auvaiyār, who is credited with 59 of the 154 poems that speak of politics, war, kings and love. The first kind of *Cankam* poetry, known as *puram*, is about public affairs, mainly the business of war, as one might expect from a warrior culture. The other type is called *akam*, which concerns itself with private experiences and reflections. Women's poetry of the *puram* category are responses to the unavoidable and therefore tragic necessity of losing husbands, sons and fathers to the ceaseless battles that defined their world. Their grief is heroic precisely because they accept its need. They mourn the loss of their loved ones intensely but they would not have it any other way. It is this pride that turns these poems into public monuments of grief, especially as they are erected in words that come from women, who are the creators and vehicles of the lives they watch slipping away. To appreciate the power of this union of resolute pride and fortitude, consider these excerpts from the *Puranānūru*, an anthology of battle poetry from *Cankam* culture:

Song of Auvaiyār:

> In the forward march of battle, with the royal drum
> enwrapped in thongs
> roaring, how can there be any victory left to be won? They
> came
> but could not stand against your vanguard. They scattered
> and they ran!
>
> (Hart and Heifetz 1999, pp. 65–6,
> poem no. 93)

Song of Kākkaipaṭiniyār Naccellaiyār:

> 'If he fled in the furious battle, I will cut off the breast
> at which he sucked!'. . . .
> And when she found her son who was scattered
> in pieces, she felt happier than she had been the day she
> bore him.
>
> (Hart and Heifetz 1999, p. 165,
> poem no. 278)

Song of Okkūr Mācāttiyār:

> . . . Her mind
> whirling, she put a spear into the hand of her only son and
> she wound
> a white garment around his body and smeared oil upon the
> dry
> topknot of his hair and having nothing
> but him said 'Go now!' and sent him off into the battle!
>
> (Hart and Heifetz 1999, p. 166,
> poem no. 279)

This is not the typical womanly stance that one might expect from the patterns of conduct we have found drawn up in the debates over women's nature and duties. Yet *cankam* society was by no means outside the Hindu world. Here again we encounter an alternative set of ideals fully functional within the Hindu worldview, evidently without friction.

If grief leads the women poets of this era to assert their strength, joy can hardly do less. That is what we discover in women's poems from the other group, known as *akam*, which voice their experience of private emotion. These poems are highly romantic in their expression of love, usually erotic and expressed through symbolic imagery drawn from nature, the seasons, and the animal world. Even the single example presented below will show the boldness and clarity of the poet's voice:

Kapilar, *Akanānūru* 332:

> **What she said to her friend**
>
> 'The man is just right
> for your rank and nature.'
> Sweet words those, bless you,
> they've come true;
> garlands smell on him
> like nectar to people who crave it,
> his chest's embrace so tight
> there's no place
> even for the waist of a bee,
> and love
> is tireless still
> as on the very first day.
>
> (Ramanujan 1985, pp. 27–8)

Centred on the human body, this poem vigorously asserts its presence in the material world of humankind and nature. The author of this poem, like those of the *puram* poems, speaks with absolute confidence in her grasp of her world, with full expectation of being heard by her equals. Their authority as poets comes from their imagination working on material rather than spiritual experience as in the case of religious poets. This secular realm too is thus peopled by women in Hindu culture.

A noteworthy woman poet writing in the secular mode is Vidyā or Vijjakā, who lived in the sixth century and wrote in Sanskrit and Prākṛt. Her imagery of nature and the human body defines moments of joy in human affections and the experience of the material world in incisively brief statements, as these examples show:

Love in Enjoyment

After my sweetheart
puts his hands to the knots of my dress,
I swear that I remember nothing.

(Ingalls 1979 [1965], p. 156, verse 574)

The Wanton

Who made your willow trees, O River Muralā . . .
to offer wantons such a chance to taste
uninterrupted love?

(Ingalls 1979 [1965], p. 188, verse 809)

Substantiations

If its roots are burned by desert sands
will the champak think to blossom?

(Ingalls 1979 [1965], p. 265, verse 1375)

From these poets of love we now turn to one similarly grounded in the experience of the world but impelled by suffering, not joy. Like Mollā, this poet from sixteenth-century Bengal, Candrāvatī, tells the *Rāmāyaṇa* story, but in an original twist she uses it to counter the celebratory masculinity of the epic. The epic tells the story of Prince Rāma and the abduction of his wife Sītā by the demon King Rāvaṇa, from whom Rāma rescues Sītā but later sends her into exile on the suspicion unjustly cast by his subjects on her chastity while in Rāvaṇa's custody. Instead of the usual glorification of Rāma's heroism, Candrāvatī tells the story from Sītā's point of view, lamenting her undeserved suffering as common to women's lot in this world. This view of women's destiny the poet further reinforces by drawing parallels to other women's lives, including Rāvaṇa's wife Mandodarī's, a lesson learned from her own tragic life.[12] Never presenting the story as a challenge to the established order, Candrāvatī leaves it as a requiem for womankind. As she puts it when she begins Sītā's tale,

> *āmār bhāgyer kathā, ki kaiba kāhinī* ।
> *vidhātā sṛjila more go, janamaduḥkhinī* । ।
>
> (Moulik 1970, p. 307)
>
> What shall I say about my fate, what story shall I narrate? The Lord of fate created me a sufferer from birth.

It is not that Candrāvatī ignores the injustice and cruelty of Sītā's banishment, for she warns of the disorder that follows when women are denied their place in the world:

> *lakṣmīchārḍā haibo rāijya go yāibo chāre khāre* ।
> *parer kathā kāne laile go nijer sarvanāś* ।
> *candrāvatī kahe, 'rām go tomār hailo buddhināś* । ।
>
> (Moulik 1970, p. 328)
>
> The kingdom will lose her Lakṣmī [prosperity] and will be ruined. Lending one's ears to other people's tales [brings about] one's own ruin. Candrāvatī says, O Rāma you have lost your sense.

But she relates misfortune to fate rather than to human action when she concludes,

> *candrāvatī kāindyā kay go kāhāro doṣ nāi* ।
> *karmaphal sukh duḥkha go dātā vidhātā gosāiṁ* । ।
>
> (Moulik 1970, p. 347)
>
> Candrāvatī says with tears, no one is to blame. The Lord of fate is the provider of happiness or suffering, the fruits of your action.

Yet her refusal to lay blame is in itself a mark of a woman's helplessness and by its reiteration it calls attention to itself as an indictment of a system that makes women so utterly dependent on men. What can Candrāvatī do? The only option she has in a world that leaves her with no power to act is to write. Writing becomes her action and as posterity has proven, it has had far greater influence than any physical act might have exerted.

I have spent some time over Candrāvatī because for her age she is a rare articulator of women's suffering under the rules of a society dominated by masculine interests. Her vision is rare because her suffering does not send her rushing to seek solace from the customary refuge of the oppressed, the compassion of gods and goddesses, but shocks her into discovering parallels in every narrative of women's lives, even that of the apotheosized Sītā.

Apart from the individuality of Candrāvatī's realization that in her world women must and will suffer simply because they are women, we must note that this critique never seems to have drawn censure from the moral arbiters of that world. Are we then to conclude that even as it laid heavy burdens on women, that world accepted contrary opinions? We know that instead of being silenced, Candrāvatī earned considerable respect from her contemporaries if the popularity of her work and the memorializing of her life are any indication. Well into the twentieth century her *Rāmāyaṇa* continued to be recited and sung in what is now Bangladesh.[13] How can we *not* rediscover here the duality in Hindu views of women that we have consistently noted in our survey of Hindu ethical literature, that is, the structural co-existence of an oppressive gender ideology and its simultaneous if muted undercutting?

The women writers we have considered in this chapter have left for us poetry that is always marked by an intensity of feeling and a close conjunction of experience and expression. They often follow literary conventions but do not let conventions dictate their self-discovery or their self-representation. As I have noted in discussing Mollā, it is not that women poets were unaware of or did not use prevailing conventions of writing. But tradition was not what they placed ahead of individuality. If you were to ask, what is the one vital and indispensable mark of women's poetry in the Hindu tradition in pre-modern times, a fair answer would be their individuality. What the discussion here has attempted to demonstrate is that they wrote not out of any desire to seek approval from the world but because they were driven by their own inner urge to make the chaos of existence meaningful, which they did either by looking closely and critically at the world around them or by discovering their own links to divinity. Whether in the religious or the secular mode, these poets have expanded the definition of womankind in the Hindu discourse of gender.

Notes

1 While no direct prohibition of education for women appears in any of the authoritative sources of Hindu social thought, there is an implicit consensus that women's duty excludes devotion to learning; see Leslie 1995 [1989], pp. 321–2.
2 Major sources for the texts used here are: *Lāllā-Vākyāni*, eds., George Grierson and Lionel D. Barnett (London: Royal Asiatic Society, 1920); Rhys-Davids and Norman 1989; Tharu and Lalitha, vol. 1, 1991; *Mīrā kī Prāmānik Padāvalī* (Hindi), ed. Bhagwandas Tiwari (Allahabad: Sahitya Bhavan, 1974); *Prācīna Pūrvavaṅga Gītikā*; Dehejia 1990; Sundaram 1987. The Bengali *Rāmāyaṇa* of Candrāvatī has not been translated yet; citations are to *Maimansiṃha Gītikā*. A very useful critical work is: Denton 2004.
3 *Bṛhaddevatā*, 2.82–4.
4 Though these poems are by Buddhist nuns, they are included here because, first, they are the earliest extant poems definitively attributable to women in India, and second, they reflect the world in which Hindu women also lived and in which expectations from women, regardless of religious affiliations, Buddhist, Jaina or Hindu, were the same.
5 See Craddock in Pintchman 2007, pp. 184–210.
6 Dehejia 1990, p. 2.
7 Dehejia 1990, pp. 21–2.
8 Ramanujan 1973, pp. 111–14.
9 Mahādevī Ākkā's poems are transliterated here from the original Kannada script as they appear in Menezes and Angadi 1973. I gratefully acknowledge Professor Anand Paranjpe's and Shrimati Sudha Ramananda's transliteration of the poems.
10 I am quoting Lāllā's original poems from the Stein B text as given in the Grierson and Barnett edition.
11 Jackson 2005, pp. 81–2.
12 Her life story, 'Candrāvatī' by Nayanchand Ghosh, is included in *Maimansiṃha Gītikā*.
13 For critical studies, see: Dev Sen in Bose 2000, pp. 183–91; and Mandakranta Bose, 'Reinventing the *Rāmāyaṇa* in Twentieth-Century Bengali Literature', *The Rāmāyaṇa Revisited* (New York: Oxford University Press, 2004), pp. 107–24.

5 Sanctuary

Women and home worship

Lakṣmī on a ritual clay platter

The home and the family have been women's primary location in the Hindu tradition, and it is women who have been responsible for home worship, including daily worship of household deities and occasional rites to keep the family in good favour with the divine powers. Today, as in the past, women's motive in these tasks is to win material benefits for the welfare of their family, or to be a devoted wife or mother. Though here, as in every other part of their lives, women put the family before themselves, these ceremonies provide room for women to act on their own.

What we have seen so far of Hindu beliefs and practices in religious, ethical and social contexts leaves little opportunity for expecting women to have much room for self-determination. It is not that all leaders of Hindu thought have been misogynic or neglectful of women. As we have seen in Chapter 2, the Hindu faith consistently locates femininity at the centre of its explanation of existence and makes the adoration of female divinities an essential part of religious life and of the quest for spiritual liberation. In Chapter 3 we have noted how controversy has raged deep and long on every conceivable issue relating to women, from their biological constitution and their moral make-up to their place in society and their rights. We have further noted the high regard in which scholarly women were held in the early phases of Hindu society. None of this, however, has arrested Hindu women's slide into powerlessness (in step, it is fair to point out, with women everywhere) till very recent times, signalled particularly by women's confinement within the home in domestic roles.

We have, however, also seen how some women have broken out of the mould on the wings of their imagination. Some of them were mystics who looked to their personal deities to reach for liberation, realizing the ecstasy of their devotion in poetry. Others, moving on the secular plane, recorded their personal engagement with their world, sometimes in joy, sometimes in pain, and sometimes even in protest against the burden of being women. Whether it was faith, passion or protest that inspired women's poetry, the motive might vary from one poet to another, but the common thread we see as we look back is that in authorship they found personal authenticity. It was by poetry's agency that they could claim a corner of the world uninvaded by its rules and expectations, a room of their own.

These were indeed exceptional individuals. The majority of women never ventured outside the set boundary of the family circle and the daily responsibilities of home life. Faithfully and unremittingly carried out, these responsibilities brought women favour and approval but earned them little authority. Despite radical changes in social life in modern times and considerable reconfiguration of family relationships brought about by those changes, women's roles and share of authority in some spheres of life remain unchanged. A good example is the indispensable task of worship rituals at home. In broad terms, this is a matter of ensuring the family's well-being by keeping the gods well disposed. In the past as well as the present, it has been women's responsibility to organize and carry out worship rituals for family prosperity, health and general success, or for specific benefits, such as a good match for daughters or the birth of a healthy child, preferably a son.

We have noted in Chapter 3 that women's participation in religious events were required in Hindu society in the Vedic age as partners to their husbands. But in later times their role changed to one more like that of assistants setting out materials, cooking sanctified food, serving priests and cleaning, rather than taking part in the core of the rituals. Few provisions existed for women to perform religious rites independently, as we have noted in the *dharmaśāstra*s and *gṛhyasūtra*s in Chapter 3. From the medieval age onwards, it was only in *tāntric* rituals that women had direct, participatory agency. For example, in *tāntric* practices a woman, preferably the mother, has the primary responsibility to initiate her son.[1] But these are esoteric rites and can hardly be considered relevant to the average woman's religious life. At some places in India an attempt has been made in recent times to give power to women to perform *yajña* but they are rare exceptions rather than rules. Obviously, spirituality should not be legislated and cannot be with any success; women as well as men follow their spiritual leanings on their own. It is not that part of religiosity that is in question here. The issue is the frequently elaborate regimen of ceremonies within the home designed to ensure a happy life for the family.

It has always been understood in all religious traditions that boons are in the keeping of divine beings. This belief has necessitated careful worship regimes in Hindu religious practice. Quite separate from the daily worship ritual, occasional rites are necessary to please or propitiate particular deities. Essential for the family's well-being, these rites – undertaken as vows – are called *vratas,* still practised in Hindu homes, especially in rural areas. This practice of taking vows to observe particular ceremonies as offerings of pleas or thanks to a deity is of ancient heritage, mentioned in the Purāṇas, for instance, in a text as old as the *Padmapurāṇa* from the beginning of the common era, and set apart as sacred rites for the home for special occasions. Practised for centuries as part of the annual calendar of home rituals, their practice has diminished in modern India with industrialization and the frequent scattering of families across the land or even overseas but many women, including educated professionals, still practise one or two *vratas*. Remarkably for a way of life in which priests hold the key to spiritual affairs, *vratas* have always been primarily managed by women, although priests or brahmins occasionally play some part in the events as performers of parts of the ceremony or the ritual recipients of alms. But even when priests are called in, women carry out the final part of the *vrata*, which consists in reading or reciting its *'kathā'*, that is, a homage of varying length in verse or prose aimed at reaffirming the audience's faith. There is no injunction against men performing *vratas* but in the historical reality of Hindu society men are rarely found undertaking any. *Vratas* are chosen, organized and directed principally by the mistress of the home with assistance from her daughters and daughters-in-law, if any. It is important to bear in mind that women perform *vratas* for the sake of the family, and the understanding that the family revolves around its male members is crucial to the effort put into the *vrata*. In that sense a *vrata* can hardly be called a liberating opportunity for women. Even so, the fact remains that women are the chief, if not the only actors in *vratas*, which thus provide a very special space reserved for women, in effect a refuge where they achieve a significant measure of self-sufficiency.

Whether this can be regarded as women's empowerment is debatable. Considering the leadership role that women take in *vratas* and drawing upon her own experience, Sanjukta Gupta concludes that this area of Hindu religiosity demonstrates the autonomy and power that women actually possess. In her view women 'are far more powerful in real life than they appear to be in religious records'.[2] There is no doubt that in virtually all *vratas* the central role is taken by women. But whether this constitutes power in the sense of self-determination is by no means beyond question. There is no historical or contemporary evidence that traditional *vratas* were actually invented or designed by women, and it is only in the performance of *vratas* that women take the leading role. What is their purpose in doing so? Let us remember that all *vratas* are prayers for specific, material benefits, not *mokṣa* or spiritual liberation. When these benefits are for individual members of the family or the family as a collective then the performer of the *vrata* is simply fitting herself into her ordained role as service provider to the family. Alternatively, the worshipper's goal might indeed be personal, such as that of securing a good husband or of bearing him sons. Though of personal advantage to the worshipper, this prioritization of the male is hard to accept as women's empowerment. A woman's status and relationships are of course matters of individual family dynamics, and in some families women may well play the role of guide or even preceptor at *vratas*. If so, then that family's culture is obviously such that the women in it already hold power and do not have to seek it through *vratas*.

It has been argued, by Gupta among others, that 'perfect chastity and loyalty to her husband accords a woman moral superiority over the other members of her family.'[3] In the same vein Vidyut Aklujkar argues for 'feminine power' by citing the instance of Anasūyā in the *Rāmāyaṇa* whose *pātivrātya*, that is, her exclusive and absolute commitment to moulding herself to her husband's needs, enabled her to control the sunrise, movements of the day and night and even that of turning powerful gods to helpless babies,[4] and who advises Sītā, 'whether he lives in the city, or he lives in the woods, whether he is evil, or he is inauspicious, the woman who loves her husband attains the best region.'[5] If these claims mean, as they seem to, that a woman may gain superiority only through *pātivrātya*, then the thesis they are propounding is one of empowerment through self-abnegation. That may be meaningful in an otherworldly context, not in social reality.

Undoubtedly, it is because in traditional Hindu society women are taught from childhood to regard selfless service as a core virtue for women that they embrace *vratas* as an indispensable duty. It is certainly legitimate to argue that the performance of a duty brings a sense of fulfilment, especially when it is for the good of those one loves. Taken in this sense the performance of *vratas* is indeed uplifting and they do provide women with a space within the family where they are mistresses of their own decision to serve and to put others before themselves. A close look at the context, structure and purpose of *vratas* will illustrate this paradox of authority gained through servitude.

But first, a few words about religion in the domestic space. Home worship can be of three kinds: the daily offering of flowers, incense, food and prayers to a family's chosen household deity, such as Kṛṣṇa, Durgā, Lakṣmī, Gaṇeśa or Śiva; these are *nitya* or everyday rituals. Then there are more elaborate celebrations of the same deities and many others on special days, complete with an extended ritual and feasting. Finally, there are the *naimittika* rituals, that is, rituals for special occasions or particular goals, and they are smaller rites targeting very specific boons, such as regaining someone's health or an easy childbirth. Strictly speaking, it is this last kind of performance that are called *vratas*. The deities worshipped are sometimes local or village deities, such as Itu, Subacanī or Manasā and sometimes major gods or goddesses, such as Śiva, Caṇḍī or Durgā, solicited on specific days for specific boons, such as securing long life for a husband, or good health for children, or safety from snakebite. Because of their local or regional currency, there are vast numbers of these rituals spread across India and some of them have crossed the oceans to command adherence among the Hindu diaspora in far-off lands. *Vratas* are wholly pragmatic in their intent and none promises *mokṣa*, liberation from birth and the ecstasy of submersion in the godhead. There are set days in the year for some *vratas* but some may be performed on any date convenient for the worshipper. Sometimes the identical deity, Lakṣmī being a prime example, may command all three kinds of worship, as we shall see later in this chapter.

For most *vratas*, the directions for choosing materials, processes and prayers are oral, handed down from older to younger women, usually from mother to daughter or daughter-in-law, and frequently some of the rules are customized by the celebrant to satisfy some conditions peculiar to her family or her own preferential emphasis. A distinctive feature of the more elaborate *vratas* is the requirement of reciting or reading out legends known as *kathā* if in prose and short, or *pāñcālī* if long, complex and in verse. These legends relate the benefits of pleasing the god or goddess who is its object, and the penalties for ignoring him or her. Since the spread of the printed word and literacy in the nineteenth century, the procedures and *pāñcālīs* of many *vratas* have been available in print but the oral tradition of individual families remains paramount in observing the details of the process.

The general structure of the *vratas* as performance events is fairly common. In the preparatory part the celebrant starts with self-purification by fasting and taking a bath, or some similar act of ablution, puts on new or clean or, preferably, silken garments, cleans the designated space for the ceremony, which could be inside the home or outside in the courtyard, sets up the deity's image if required – often made out of clay by the celebrant or painted on a clay platter – and sets out the ritual materials, such as a consecrated water pot, flowers, food items, clothing, lamps and incense. Celebrants then begin the actual series of actions, such as offering the deity the prescribed material, such as flowers, food and water, usually to the chanting of verses composed specifically for this *vrata* and handed down from generation to generation. After the offerings and chanting, the *kathā* or *pāñcālī* recording the deity's legend is narrated. The *vrata* concludes with the distribution of the consecrated food, and for some *vratas*, alms to brahmins. For *vratas* that require formal worship processes, priests have to be engaged but most require none, although giving alms to brahmins is fairly common.

Variations on this general pattern are infinite and made to fit the needs of individual *vratas*, determined by the celebrant's assumption of what might be most efficacious for the particular deity. These variations are hard to account for but seem to be derived either from the legend or from some circumstance of the celebrant's family history or needs. For instance, for the same *vrata* some families use a clay icon while some use a painted clay platter. The rationale behind selecting a deity for worshipping or for selecting the materials for the ritual is usually obscure; for instance, there is no obvious reason why blessings particularly for newly-weds should be sought from the goddess Subacanī, who rules over geese. Again, there is no explanation for stipulating the use of seventeen grains of rice, seventeen blades of grass, and seventeen handfuls of rice cooked in milk in the *Rāldurgā vrata*.

A particularly noteworthy element in the process of *vratas* is the requirement of physical preparation on the celebrant's part in the form of fasting and bathing (or an equivalent). Both are designed to ensure self-cleansing leading to the purity of the body. Physical purity is of enormous importance in Hindu culture, especially in the form of avoidance of pollution. For women this is of particular significance because, traditionally, maintaining the purity of the home has been largely women's responsibility. To move to a related though deeper philosophical view of society, we may remember what Arjuna says to Kṛṣṇa in the *Bhagavadgītā*:

> *strīṣu duṣṭāṣu vārṣṇeya jāyate varṇasaṃkaraḥ* | |
>
> (*Bhagavadgītā*, 1.41)
>
> Through corrupt women, Vārṣṇeya [Kṛṣṇa], comes miscegenation.

The purpose or performance of *vratas* may not be directly related to the perception of so public a crisis. But the fact that *vratas* demand strict bodily purity from celebrants, who are almost always women, places these rituals in line with the ideology of Hinduism's most influential text.

It is impossible to say which *vrata* started when but they have survived the tumults of India's history and continue to be practised all over India, although every region has its specially popular *vratas*.

For instance, women from all walks of life in the Hindi speaking areas of Northern India observe the *Karvā Chauth vrata*. A fast kept by women to win longevity for their husbands and for conjugal love, this *vrata* is not commonly practised in other regions. In South India the month-long *Pāvai vrata* is observed by young maidens to secure happy and long-lasting married lives. *Ekādaśī vrata* is observed by widowed women to gain peace in the afterlife since they have nothing left in their present lives to look forward to. The *Sāvitrī vrata* is observed in the month of *jaiṣṭha* (mid-May to mid-June) by married women for fourteen years to avoid widowhood. A popular *vrata* of Bengali Hindus is the *Ṣaṣṭhī vrata* observed two to six times a year, depending on regional variations, by mothers for the welfare of their children.[6]

Familiarization with *vratas* begins at an early age. A good example from Bengal is the *daśaputtali vrata* celebrated by five-year-old girls in the hope of finding a caring husband and marrying into a good family. This long-drawn *vrata* begins at the end of the Bengali calendar year. After taking a bath every morning for a month from the last day of *caitra* to the last day of *vaiśākha* (mid-April to mid-May), each young celebrant draws a circular pattern, an *ālpanā*, consisting of ten female figures with rice paste on earth. To each figure she offers flowers, *tulasī* and *dūrvā* grass while reciting:

ebār pūjoy bar nebo *rāmer mata pati pābo*
ebār pūjoy bar nebo *sītār mata satī habo*
ebār pūjoy bar nebo *lakṣmaṇer mata deor pābo*
ebār pūjoy bar nebo *daśarather mata śvaśur pābo*
ebār pūjoy bar nebo *kauśalyār mata śvāśuḍī pābo*
ebār pūjoy bar nebo *kuntīr mata putravatī habo*
ebār pūjoy bar nebo *draupadīr mata rādhunī habo*
ebār pūjoy bar nebo *durgār mata śakti pābo*
ebār pūjoy bar nebo *pṛthivīr mata bhār sabo*
ebār pūjoy bar nebo *ṣaṣṭhīr mata jeoñj habo*

With this *pūjā* I ask for a boon to get a husband like Rāma,
With this *pūjā* I ask for a boon to be a *satī* like Sītā,
With this *pūjā* I ask for a boon to get a brother-in-law like Lakṣmaṇa,
With this *pūjā* I ask for a boon to get a father-in-law like Daśaratha,
With this *pūjā* I ask for a boon to get a mother-in-law like Kausalyā,
With this *pūjā* I ask for a boon to be a mother like Kuntī,

With this *pūjā* I ask for a boon to be as good a cook as Draupadī,
With this *pūjā* I ask for a boon to be as powerful as Durgā,
With this *pūjā* I ask for a boon to be able to bear burdens like Pṛthivī [the earth],
With this *pūjā* I ask for a boon to be able to bear long-lived children like Ṣaṣṭhī.

This *vrata* and the others briefly noted above are uniformly directed towards securing the bliss of a life that revolves around a good marriage and its happy consequences. But there are also examples of much more ambitious *vratas* that are aimed at securing not just these but every other material benefit. One of the most potent of such *vratas* is the multilayered regimen for the worship of Lakṣmī, the goddess of wealth, beauty and a contented family life. By tracing the progress of her worship through the year we may see how extensive the programme is for seeking her benefaction.

As one might expect where the presiding deity of worldly good is concerned, Lakṣmī is worshipped frequently and fervently. Her rites are performed by married women who offer her *pūjā* at home every day, and more extensively, every week on Thursdays (a *nitya* or regular affair). A more elaborate observance occurs in the month of *bhādra* in the late monsoon. The principal annual (or *vārṣika*) celebration takes place every autumn as part of the month-long celebration of the Great Goddess Durgā, Lakṣmī being her daughter. This occasion for worshipping Lakṣmī requires a brahmin priest as it includes a formal *pūjā* including a *yajña* and because its complexity calls for a professional, although much of its conduct is the responsibility of women. Added to these are rites aimed at special (*naimittika*) occasions to win specific benefactions. A very important part of the worship process is the reciting of celebratory legends, although they are not necessary for the daily observance.

The procedure for the regular daily *pūjā* is fairly simple: after taking a bath in the morning, the mistress of the house puts on a fresh *sārī*, preferably a silken one, which is supposed to be the purest fabric. She cleans the shrine and the prayer room every day, also bathing the image of Lakṣmī and putting on fresh garments. She places in front of the deity a small water-pot made of silver, copper or brass, filled with water (from the Ganges where possible) and with a fruit on top. She offers plates of fruits and sweets, a glass of water, flowers, unhusked rice, *dūrvā* grass, black sesame seed, vermillion, a lighted lamp and incense and finally says her prayer. On Thursdays the process takes longer and is usually attended by an audience who are required to listen to *Lakṣmīr pāñcālī* while holding in their hands flower and *dūrvā* grass offerings, followed by the distribution of sweets. This basic pattern of action is common to all celebrations of the goddess but annual or special *vratas* take on more details.

In addition to these daily and weekly rituals, some women also take a vow to offer a special *pūjā* to the goddess in the months of *bhādra* (mid-August to mid-September), *kārtika* (mid-October to mid-November), *pauṣa* (mid-December to mid-January), and *caitra* (mid-March to mid-April). One may choose any one or all of these special months to carry out this *vrata*. These broader versions of the *vrata* require all of the duties prescribed for the basic daily rituals plus several others. For instance, the celebrants have to draw a special *ālpanā* (design on the floor with rice paste)[7] under the water-pot in front of the image, a *pañcapallava* (five-leaf mango spray) covering the mouth of the pot, with a fruit on top. Certain variations in the process differentiate the seasonal performances but the core of the pattern remains the same. For instance, the *vrata* performed in *bhādra* concludes with the recitation of a shorter *kathā* or tale by the mistress of the household who performs the *vrata* rather than the longer *Lakṣmīr pāñcālī* recited at other occasions.

The tale told at the *bhādra* celebration is about a poor Brahmin widow and her son. Through her dedication and faith in Lakṣmī and by observing this *vrata*, she received the goddess's blessings and prospered. Her son was generous and gave his own food to Goddess Lakṣmī's favourite ride, an owl, which pleased her even more. When the time came for her to leave this world, the brahmin woman advised her son and daughter-in-law to continue with this *pūjā* and to recite this tale in order to ensure the continuation of their good fortune.

The principal occasion for worshipping Lakṣmī is the annual *pūjā* called *Kojāgarī Lakṣmī Pūjā*, which is performed on the night of the full-moon after the annual autumn *Durgāpūjā*. This is specially celebrated by married Bengali Hindu women. In many households a clay image specially fashioned for this annual *pūjā* is bought just for this occasion and kept at home for a year after being worshipped, while the image from the previous year is sent for immersion the next evening after bidding her a ritual farewell. The celebration, performed at the juncture of afternoon and evening, is elaborate and its important portions are conducted by a brahmin priest to the accompaniment of Sanskrit *mantras*. Essential features of the ceremony are fasting through the day, preparing food for the goddess and the family and guests, drawing Goddess Lakṣmī's footprints in rice paste across the floor to indicate her presence in the home, and decorating the entire house with auspicious *ālpanā* as part of the festivity. Fruits, sweets, flowers, unhusked rice, black sesame seed and *dūrvā* grass are also offered to the image, followed by the recitation of the *pāñcālī* by the mistress of the family. She does all of this with help from young daughters and daughters-in-law of the family. Women of the household are expected to stay up all night under the moonlit sky listening to the *vratakathā* read out by the mistress of the household. It is compulsory to have these readings at the end of the ceremony after the priest leaves, for without them the *pūjā* remains incomplete.

The difference between the Lakṣmī *vratakathā* and *pāñcālī* is substantial although their intent is the same. The first is a tale of the misfortunes that a king suffers because he finds himself forced to entertain the goddess Alakṣmī, Lakṣmī's ill-willed counterpart (also known as her elder sister) but is restored to his fortune when his queen begins to perform the *Lakṣmī vrata*. This *pūjā* assures the blessings of *kulalakṣmī* (Lakṣmī who rules over the family) for family contentment, of *bhāgyalakṣmī* (Lakṣmī who rules over fate) for good fortune, and of *yaśolakṣmī* (Lakṣmī who rules over fame) for fame.

The Lakṣmī *pāñcālī* is a much longer and better known story which is also much more theologically oriented. It begins in the heavenly abode of Viṣṇu and Lakṣmī, who laments that the world is being overwhelmed by the dereliction of duty and propriety, especially by women. The only way to save the world is to worship Lakṣmī faithfully, the alternative being the loss of wealth, fame and fortune, as illustrated by the life of two different merchant families. The first of them suffers misfortune when the sons of the family are led by their wives into conflict; but their fortune is recovered when their old mother is instructed by Lakṣmī herself to pray to her. The second story is about a merchant who is too proud to respect Lakṣmī, about whose power he says:

> *kapāle nā thāke yadi lakṣmī debe dhan!*
> *hena vākya kabhu āmi śunini kakhan!*
>
> Lakṣmī will bless me with wealth even if fate does not!
> I have never heard such a tale!

Annoyed by these sneering words, the goddess abandons him and his family to abject poverty. After some time, when he sees the women of a rich family performing this *vrata*, he realizes his mistake and tells his wife and daughters-in-law to perform it, concluding his account with a long *stuti* of Lakṣmī, that is, a formal composition in adoration of her greatness. After his wife and the rest of the family perform the *vrata* faithfully, the goddess restores the merchant's wealth and he lives happily ever after with his family.

A crucial aspect of both narratives is the weight given to women. The unfortunate (though righteous) king recovers his fortune when his queen worships Lakṣmī. Similarly, the quarrelling brothers fall into misfortune because they are incited by their wives but recover when their mother persuades the same wicked wives to turn to Lakṣmī. Again, in the arrogant merchant's tale, the living example of the way to regain Lakṣmī's favour is supplied by the women of a right-thinking family, while the actual process of recovery is undertaken by the merchant's wife and daughters-in-law. In these tales women are the transforming agents even though they act under the direction of others.

Tracing the performance of this *vrata* shows how meticulously its process and its narrative are designed to make its promise believable. The logic of the narrative is particularly important as a play between threat and promise: if you do this, you will have the best of life; if you neglect it, you will suffer. At the same time, the narrative is careful also to intimate that even neglect is not an irreversible fault. The goddess is ever merciful and easily placated. The actual performance process again underlines the simplicity and ease of propitiating her; at its most basic, the *vrata* requires just a few items and none too costly or hard to get. Clearly, the elementary reasoning and modest material requirements of the *vrata* are crucial to its acceptance. The appeal and threat to self-interest on the one hand and accessibility on the other are significant features of this and similar *vratas*, placing them at the core of popular Hinduism, the location of which is the family. It is because within the family women are the most active actors even when they are not its first citizens, that *vratas* enable women to carve out a territory of their own.

Notes

1 See Gupta in Leslie 1989, pp. 208–9, citing the *Prāṇatoṣiṇī Tantra*, ch. 2.
2 See Gupta, 'The Goddess, Women, and Their Rituals in Hinduism', in Bose 2000, p. 96; and June McDaniel, 'Does Tantric Ritual Empower Women? Renunciation and Domesticity among Female Bengali Tantrikas', in Pintchman 2007, pp. 227–54.
3 Gupta, in Bose 2000, p. 96.
4 Aklujkar, 'A Pativratā with Panache', in Bose 2000, pp. 56–68.
5 Aklujkar, in Bose 2000, p. 57.

6 Professor Malashri Lal of Delhi University in a recent lecture (13 March 2009) at the University of British Columbia said that *Karvā Chauth* is observed by female professors, housewives and orthodox families in Delhi today. It is a very popular *vrata* in that region. Among Bengali middle class educated women in West Bengal the practice of *Śivarātri vrata,* which is meant for the welfare of husbands or for getting good husbands, has dwindled but the *vrata* remains important in popular practice. A large number of Bengali widows everywhere continue to observe *ekādaśī.* As for *Pāvai* in Tamilnadu, it is still practised by many young women.

7 In South India every morning the mistress of the household draws auspicious designs with rice-powder, *kolam,* at the entrance of her home.

6 Conclusion

> The Hindu discourse on womankind is vast and more often divisive than not. The provisions for women's life in traditional thought are many and generally restrictive, especially when backed by religious ideology. Setting goddesses and mortal women side by side shows how Hindu thought has historically conflated power and dependency within the idea of womanhood, no matter how irreconcilable the two positions might be. Still more intriguing is that the seemingly inescapable dependency that such a belief system imposes on women has also provided room for liberation through acts of creative imagination within the conditions of its religious culture.

As the previous chapters have pointed out, this study directs its audience primarily to Hindu thought rather than social practice relating to women. It will also have been clear that the purpose of this study is not to offer an exposition of Hindu philosophical ideas except where they relate to ideas of gender, most prominently in the linkages between women and Hindu goddesses. While we need to acknowledge that in matters of lived experience, thought and practice are indeed interdependent and that thought determines practice as much as practice gives rise to ideas, we can take only one of these categories at a time for the sake of concentrated and fruitful attention. That is why this study begins by assembling textual material that reflects the views of Hindu thinkers on women. A striking characteristic, and perhaps a troubling one, of the material presented in this study is the frequent self-contradiction within texts. The *Manusmṛti* and the *Mahābhārata* are good cases in point, containing as they do both praise and dispraise for women. But we have to remember that these texts are compilations of opinions gathered over time rather than the unified works of single authors, and it is their variety that underscores the controversial character of the Hindu discourse on women. The views that comprise that discourse tend to be generalizations whose roots in experience, if any, remain unstated, as is the reasoning behind them. Why, for instance, does the *Mahābhārata* say that women are 'pure, sacred, and lights of our homes', or what accounts for the *Ṛg Veda*'s condemnation of women as possessing 'hearts like those of hyenas'? Only in rare instances is an opinion derived from some material observation, which, while it might be indefensible in fact, may be at least an attempt to argue on the basis of observation and reason. The argument by Baudhāyana and Vasiṣṭha that no sin can possibly attach to women because their bodies are cleansed at regular intervals by menstruation is bad science but is nonetheless an attempt to find some sort of reason for an opinion, however unsound the reasoning may be. But assessing the soundness of an opinion is less our concern here than the attitude it represents and the trend of thought to which it contributes.

Perhaps more important than particular points of view or even broad attitudes, as I have noted at several points in this study, is the endless concern of Hindu thinkers with women as a subject of study and social policy. The female character and the female body have been targets of such intense scrutiny that one begins to wonder whether to the majority of scholars, lawgivers and leaders of Hindu society women did not appear to be an altogether different species from males. It is this sense of intrinsic difference that underlies the speculation, frequently intemperate to the point of misogyny, about women's nature. And that sense of essential difference runs even through more balanced views and regulates women's place in society. We must note here that where women's social location is concerned, the context is the family, which is viewed without question as women's primary scene of action, for nowhere in the long discussion of women's roles are women envisioned in non-familial social relationships, such as those dictated by affairs of commerce or by civic and state institutional roles. Keeping the discussion centred on women as a species tightly enclosed within the family meant an uncompromising idealization of women's lives and functions to the exclusion of concrete social life. Was this because in traditional Hindu society women simply did not have non-familial social positions? But that is hardly borne out by history, especially the historical testimony of literature, which does tell us of women engaged in activities outside the family, notably in the labour force and small trade. Even in pre-modern India, women who worked as labourers or shopkeepers did spend a large part of their lives outside the family. In his *Arthaśāstra* Kauṭilya makes particular provision for female workers and artisans under the Supervisor of Weaving.[1] To take a minor but common example from early Indian literature, a familiar figure of civic life in early times was the *mālinī*, or female flower-seller, who could be either an independent tradesperson or a keeper of the royal garden. Such entirely real figures are never acknowledged in the Hindu discourse on women, which suggests that 'woman' as a category is a theoretical construction providing the templates for women's character attributes and functions in real life. It was through this normative exercise that ideology came to determine practice.

This emphasis on the family shows not only a systematic attempt at containment but also the need for a stable institution at the centre of community life. In this the Hindu thinkers of early times were no different from their modern counterparts or from social philosophers in other cultures throughout time. But in the Hindu context the insistence upon domesticating women within an elaborate web of family roles and duties requires so complete a submersion of the individual in the needs of the family collective that self-sacrifice becomes the highest possible duty. It is not that putting family before self was not enjoined upon men. Sacrificing personal aspirations or even simple needs to family interests has remained a much-lauded ideal for individuals, men as well as women, in Hindu society from early ages till now and is just one facet of the overarching exaltation of self-sacrifice as perhaps the highest social virtue held up to a Hindu. But while the Hindu ethic leaves open for a man many arenas of worldly action – the home, the marketplace, the court, the battlefield – in which to prove his moral worth, for a woman it is solely the home where her virtue, understood as self-sacrifice, must shine.

Let us note once again that it is not only in Hindu ethics that domesticity is exalted as women's crowning virtue. Well into the industrial age Western social ideology acclaimed that particular virtue as a woman's chief glory, as Coventry Patmore's well-known effusions on the 'Angel in the House' (1854) testifies. But Hindu thought is far more complex than a straightforward patriarchal strategy to discipline women by ideological manipulation. The containment of women within the network of duties to the family that Hindu thought has woven lies rooted in a deeper, darker and essentially metaphysical conception of existence rather than a sociological one. This is evident in the ever-renewed linkages between women and goddesses. As we have seen in Chapter 3, Hindu goddesses are cast in the mould of mortal women and caught in the same web of familial relationships as wives, daughters and mothers. Even the most powerful goddesses are consorts, and while that does not necessarily make them dependent upon their spouses, it defines their power and their wielding of it in terms of family roles.

But Hindu ideas about women do not halt at the domestication of the feminine, whether divine or mortal. At a deep level of response there is an ever-present sense of menace correlated with femininity which expresses itself in the Hindu imagination as the conception of destructive goddesses, best represented by Kālī but by no means alien to benign figures, including the benevolent Mother Goddess who, we may remember, also resorts to violence, albeit for the protection of her children. That divine beings, male and female alike, should have superhuman powers, including the power of destruction is not a matter of surprise. What is surprising is that the Hindu pantheon should accommodate so many female figures who, even though they are always conceived within family relationships and in tandem with their male consorts, stand directly opposite benevolent goddesses such as Lakṣmī, who embody tender, selfless and bountiful altruism. This opposition mirrors the contradiction that runs through the pronouncements on women we have examined in Chapter 3 where derogatory views of women's supposedly essential nature stand in puzzling contrast to paeans to women's inalienable and life-giving virtue.

When we consider this duality of conception of the divine female as both benign and malevolent, we begin to suspect, even without getting into psychological, especially Freudian, theories of masculine responses to the feminine, that there is a strong sense of the unknowable and therefore fearsome mystery in which the feminine is implicated. In our discussion on Hindu goddesses we have seen how their benevolent attributes are extended to the idealized woman. Would we be unjustified in seeing a parallel extension of the destructive force of Hinduism's terrifying goddesses to mortal women? But bear in mind that we have also seen this traffic of defining attributes flowing not only from heaven to earth but equally from earth to heaven since a goddess may be conceived as the quintessence of an idealized woman. Just as a woman of exemplary virtue who augments the wealth of her family by her good management and selfless service might be thought of as Lakṣmī, so might the goddess, as imagined by devotees, be a distilled form of that woman's character. It is as likely that goddesses are idealizations of women as that women are pale shadows of goddesses conceived as the idealized feminine. Similarly, the conception of the destructive goddesses of Hinduism may well be personifications of men's fear of women. The reason for it is a matter of psychological explanation, as I have said above, and it is hard to prove that there is in fact such fear, but it is too well attested in anthropological literature to be ignored.[2] It is thus a hypothesis that addresses the ambivalence implicit in the side-by-side existence of life-giving and death-dealing goddesses. Imagining powerful goddesses is a recognition of the destructive potential assigned to women, fully realized in Kālī, but implicit in the Mother Goddess. In human society the response to such feminine power is a call for deflection, constraint and erasure in the interest of the stability of community life as conceived under patriarchal systems, all of which are achieved by containing women within family relationships and household duties.

Such containment is achieved as much by precept as by example. Not only are there explicit injunctions, as we have seen in Chapter 3, for women to play the role of subservient wife, selfless mother and tireless housekeeper, but also legends that reinforce the benefits of compliance, set off by dire examples of the consequences of non-compliance. These roles are not imposed upon goddesses but they are assumed to be models of conduct illustrated by the benevolent goddesses, to be emulated by women on earth. The set of ideals we are considering covers both human and divine females, correlating women and goddesses through interchangeable personae.

Obviously, goddesses and women are placed on different platforms of power. Yet even here one may discern continuity. Goddesses, after all, are defined by their relationship with male consorts or their children, which places them in roles of dependency. Conversely, women do exert authority upon members of their families through the respect they gain as nurturing mother or virtuous wife. They may command obedience as the performer of *vratas* that ensure the family's welfare, as we have seen in Chapter 5. In extreme cases a woman may even be revered as a *devī*; indeed, the term is commonly used in Hindu society as a mark of deep respect for a woman. The irony here is that Hindu thought invests the virtuous woman with authority even as it subjects her to self-erasing duty. By setting goddesses and mortal women within a shared framework, Hindu thought has historically conflated power and dependency within the idea of womanhood, no matter how irreconcilable the two positions might be. We must also recognize that the lure of gaining authority by self-sacrifice, most dramatically demonstrated by the institution of *satī*, is in itself a call to bondage, masked though it may be in the rhetoric of noble fortitude and altruism.

Considering the straitjacket of prescribed rules on the one hand and cultural enticement on the other that we have been discussing, we may well ask, is there no alternative to this scheme of women's life in Hindu thought and practice? The apparent answer is, no, there is not. But it is a superficial answer as quick judgements usually are. We are speaking here of course in the context of traditional Hindu society and in that context women are indeed locked into roles defined by those rules. At the same time we must also recognize that the seemingly inescapable dependency imposed by such a belief system on women has also provided room for liberation through acts of creative imagination within the conditions of its religious and social culture. As we have seen in our study of women poets in Chapter 4, Hindu thought has room not only for domesticated females, mortal and divine, but also for women who leave the mundane world for a spiritual life as well as women who critique social conditions.

But before we rush to cite the lives of these women as refutation of women's subordination in Hindu thought, let us not forget that such women are exceptions. It is not likely that renunciation would be approved in Hindu thought (or in any other social milieu) as a desirable choice for women. The texts of Hindu law and custom examined in Chapter 3 leave little room for doubt that women as a biological category are strictly defined and their lives as social creatures hedged around by rules for every occasion. Nevertheless it is also part of the same Hindu reality that women renunciates are revered in thought and practice, their poems and songs held high in popular appeal and their lives sanctified for posterity even when in life they may have been persecuted by their male cohorts, as Mīrābāi was.

As we consider the lives and works of the women poets it becomes clear that they are an anomaly in the scheme of gender roles that evolved in Hindu thought. Many of the women represented in Chapter 4 did face persecution when they began to look for spiritual fulfilment outside their pre-ordained roles within the family or even to repudiate the physical conventions imposed by their gender identity by, for instance, throwing aside clothes, as did Mahādevī Ākkā and Lāllā. History does not tell us how many such women were cowed into submission and returned to their appointed places but some refused to surrender. Their surrender was to their self-chosen god, as we see in the poems cited here. The trade-off was liberation from the regimentation of ordinary social life whose arbiters, in the kind of ironic about-face so frequent in the history of Hindu society, sanctified these same women as beings existing above the common dust.

The other irony in the lives of these saintly women is that in their poetry they constantly imagine their intense personal relationship to god in terms of domesticity. The god worshipped is the speaker's lover and husband. Her yearning to be united with him takes on the flavour of a romantic passion expressed in the rhetoric of conjugality, as we have seen in the excerpts from Mahādevī and Mīrā. This may suggest that even on this plane the poets are unable to escape their bondage to the family as an institution. But the crucial difference is that there is in fact no bondage, for the human-divine relationship is never one of coercion, nor one imposed upon the subject by her world, but one chosen independently. Nor are these forms of familial address confined to women poets. It is not even typical of the Hindu spiritual tradition but common to many traditions of mysticism and adopted by women as well as men. In the Hindu idiom, the commonest term for addressing and imagining a goddess is 'Mother', as we see in the songs, among those of countless others, of the hugely popular nineteenth-century poet of eastern India, Ramprasad Sen, whose work we have briefly noted in Chapter 2. Such poets, male or female, yearn to reach out for the spirit, not a physical entity, for, as the nineteenth-century religious philosopher and reformer Swami Vivekananda was fond of saying, the soul has no gender. The familial mode is no more than a metaphoric matrix of rapture and a tool for capturing through the imagination the utterly unimaginable.

The acceptance, indeed the high status of the women poets within Hindu society is as crucial as the texts of Hindu law and social usage to understanding the Hindu discourse of gender. The socially determined rigour of women's lives as conceptualized in the religious and ethical texts is at sharp variance with the freedom that the women religious poets wrest from their world by rejecting human authority over their lives. The astonishing paradox that the same ethical system should accommodate both inflexible regulation and their wholesale rejection may be the reason why that system survived through centuries of challenge and social turmoil from within and outside. Not the least of these challenges continued to come from its arbiters throughout the history of Hindu society. Against downright misogyny the tradition produced unambiguous endorsements of women's innate nature and on the level of practical, everyday life provided for safeguards against repression. The history of Hindu thought concerning women thus shows two opposite trends, one restrictive and the other liberal.

Another reason for the longevity of Hinduism's woman-oriented ethic is that it makes provisions for so wide a range of situations and relationships in which women can be envisaged that to follow set formulas of belief and practice becomes an easy option and discourages resistance. The ideals formulated for women, restrictive at best and oppressive at worst, answer to every demand that the world can make of women and provide them with identities that they can assume at every stage of life. This pervasive idealization working through extreme regimentation is in itself a denial of liberty, especially as it is reinforced by a rhetoric that glorifies compliance. Despite the continuing impulse of liberalization, the dominant force in the Hindu discourse of women has been one of overbearing control. As an ideological apparatus that discourse has been instrumental in holding Hindu society together as a stable institution, albeit at the cost of women's disenfranchisement. Yet, as in other areas of the social structure, the historically demonstrated capacity of Hindu gender ideology for accommodating intellectual dissent has always contained the potential for change, as this study has attempted to show. The present does arise from the past; to what degree and in which areas of life the present condition of Hindu women derives from the past are questions to which this study attempts to provide answers.

Notes

1 *Kauṭilya's Arthaśāstra*, pp. 128, 129.
2 For the western context, see Ruether c2005.

Bibliography

Textual sources

Aitareya Brāhmaṇam, vol. 3. Delhi: Naga Prakashaka, 1991 [1942].

Aśvaghoṣa. *The Saundarānanda of Aśvaghoṣa*, ed. E. H. Johnston. Delhi: Motilal Banarsidass, 1975 [1928].

Atharvaveda Saṃhitā, vol. 2, *kāṇḍas* 4–6, ed. and tr. Svami S. P. Sarasvati. New Delhi: Veda Pratisthana, 1992.

The Atharva Veda, ed. and tr. Devi Chand. Delhi: Munshiram Manoharlal, 1990 [1982].

Bāṇabhaṭṭa. *The Harṣacarita of Bāṇabhaṭṭa*, ed. P. V. Kane. Delhi: Motilal Banarsidass, 1973 [1918].

Bṛhadārṇyaka Upaniṣad, ed. E. Roer. Osnabruck: Biblio Verlag, 1980 [Calcutta: Asiatic Society of Bengal, 1849–56]; Delhi: Bharatiya Kala Prakashan, 2000.

Bṛhaddevatā (attributed to Śaunaka), ed. Ramkumar Rai. Kashi Sanskrit Series, 164. Varanasi: Chaukhamba Sanskrit Samsthan, 1989.

Brahmavaivartapurāṇa, ed. J. L. Shastri. Introduction and Index by Satkari Mukhopadhyaya. Vol. 1. Delhi: Motilal Banarsidass, 2004.

Brahmavaivartapurāṇa, vols. 1 and 2, ed. Shri Ram Sharma Acharya. Bareli: Samskriti Samsthan, 1970.

Bṛhaspatismṛti, (reconstructed text), ed. K. V. Aiyangar. Baroda: Gaekwad Oriental Series, no. 85, 1941.

Baudhāyanadharmasūtram, ed. Pandit Chinnaswami Sastri. Benares City: Kashi Sanskrit Series 104, 1934.

Bhāsa. *Cārudattam*, ed. Kapiladeva Giri. Varanasi: Choukhamba Vidya Bhavan, 1966.

Devī Bhāgavata Purāna, vols. 1 and 2, ed. Ramsharma Acharya. Bareli: Samskriti Samsthan, 1968.

Devīmāhātmyam with the commentary of Nilāmbarācārya, ed. M. L. Wadekar. Vadodara: Oriental Institute, 1997.

Dharmasūtras: The Law Codes of Āpastamba, Gautama, Baudhāyana and Vasiṣṭha, ed. and tr. Patrick Olivelle. Delhi: Motilal Banarsidass, 2000.

Durgāsaptaśatī, ed. Ramesvara Bhatta. Bombay: Venkatesvara Press, 1972.

Durgāsaptaśatī, ed. Dipak Kumar Sharma. Delhi: New Bharatiya Book Corporation, 2000.

Gobhila Gṛhyasutra with Sanskrit commentary of Pt. S. Samashrami, tr. Thakur U. N. Singh. Delhi: Choukhamba Sanskrit Pratisthan, 1992 [reprint].

Jayadeva. *The Gītagovinda of Jayadeva: Love Song of the Dark Lord*, ed. and tr. Barbara Stoler Miller. Delhi: Motilal Banarsidass, 1984 [1977].

Jñānārṇavatantra, ed. Daṇḍisvāmī Dāmodara Āśrama. Calcutta: Nava Bharata Publishers, 1982.

Kālidāsa. *Abhijñānaśakuntalam*, ed. M. R. Kale. 1994 [1898].

Kālikāpurāṇam, eds. Panchanana Tarkaratna and Shrijiva Nyayatirtha. Calcutta: Nababharata Publishers, 1977.

Kauṭilya. *Arthaśāstra of Kauṭilya*, ed. and tr. Vacaspati Gairola. Varanasi: Chowkhamba Vidya Bhawan, 1962.

The Kauṭilya Arthaśāstra: *A Critical Edition with A Glossary*, ed. R. P. Kangle. 2 vols. Bombay: University of Bombay, 1960.

Kauṭilya's Arthaśāstra, tr. R. Shamasastry. Mysore: Mysore Printing and Publishing House, 1967 [1915].

Kṛttibāsa. *Kṛttibāsī Rāmāyaṇa*, ed. Harekrishna Mukhopadhyaya. Calcutta: Sahitya Samsad, 1989.

Kṛṣṇayajurvedīya Taittirīyasaṃhitā. Hariyana: Ram Lal Kapur Trust, 1982.

Kulārṇavatantra: Readings and Text, eds. M. K. Pandit and T. Vidyaratna. Madras: Ganesh & Co. (Madras) Private Limited, 1965.

Kulārṇavatantram, ed. Upendrakumar Das. Calcutta: Nava Bharata Publishers, 1976.

The Mahābhārata. Poona: Bhandarkar Oriental Research Institute, 1933–40.

The Mahābhārata, ed. Ramnarayan Shastri. Gorakhpur: Gita Press, 1964.

Mahābhāratam, ed. Haridas Siddhantavagish Bhattacharya. Calcutta: Vishvavani Prakashani, 1931.

Mahānirvāṇatantra, ed. Baldeo Prasad Misra. Bombay: Srivenkateswar Steam Press, 1985.

Maimansiṃha Gītikā, ed. Sukhamay Mukhopadhyay. Calcutta: Bharati Book Stall, 1970.

Manusmṛti, vols. 1 and 2, ed. Gangaram Jha. Delhi: Parimal Publications, 1992.

Manusmṛti, vol. 2, ed. Gangaram Jha. Calcutta: Royal Asiatic Society, 1939.

The Matsyamahāpurāṇam. Foreword by H. H. Wilson. Arranged by Nag Sharan Singh. 2 vols. Delhi: Nag Publishers, 1983.

The Matsyapurāṇa, vols. 1 and 2, tr. Sriram Sharma Acharya. Bareli: Samskriti Samsthan, 1970.

Nāradasmṛti. Text and Studies, no. 84, ed. Dr. Heramba Chatterjee Śāstrī. 2 vols. Calcutta: Sanskrit College, 1988–9.

Nāradīya Dharmaśāstra, or, *The Institutes of Nārada*, tr. Julius Jolly. London: Trübner & Co., 1876.

Niruktam: Yāska's Nirukta, ed. Amareswara Thakur. Calcutta: Calcutta University, 1955.

Pañcatantram, tr. and comm. Shri Shyamacharan Pandeya. Delhi: Motilal Banarsidass, 1975.

Parāśara. *Parāśarasmṛti*, ed. Alaka Sukla. Delhi: Parimal Publications, 1990.

Prācīna Pūrvavaṅga Gītikā, vol. 7, ed. Kshitish Moulik. Calcutta: Firma K. L. Mukhopadhyaya, 1970.

The Rāmāyaṇa: Rāmprasādī Jagadrāmī Rāmāyaṇa, in eight parts. Calcutta: Mahesh Library, 1999.

Ṛksuktaśatī, ed. and tr. H. D. Velankar. Bombay, Bharatiya Vidya Bhavan, 1972.

ṚgVeda Saṃhitā, ed. Shivnath Ahitagni. Delhi: Naga Prakashaka, 1991 [1904].

ṚgVeda Saṃhitā, vol. 2, tr. and comm. T. V. K. Sastry and M. P. Pandit. Pondicherry: Aurobinda Ashram, 1967.

ṚgVeda Saṃhitā, Mandalas 1–10, ed. K. L. Joshi. Varanasi: Chaukhamba Orientalia, 2000.

Śaktisaṅgamatantra, Tārākhaṇḍa, vol. 2, ed. Benoytosh Bhattacharya. Baroda: Bhandarkar Oriental Research Institute, 1941.

Śatapatha Brāhmaṇa, ed. and tr. William Calland. Delhi: Motilal Banarsidass, 1983.

Śrautapāṭha, coll. Pandit Sitaram Shastri. Calcutta: University of Calcutta, 1957 [1942].

Śrī Garuḍamahāpurāṇam, ed. Sri Damodar Satvalekar. Haryana: Ramlal Kapur Trust, 1984.

Śrīmaddevībhāgavatapurāṇam, vol. 1, ed. Pushpendu Kumar, tr. Raibahadur Shrischandra. Delhi: Eastern Book Linkers, 2006.

Śrī Padmamahāpurāṇam, ed. Govinda Shastri. 3 vols. Bombay: Venkateswara Press, 1927.

Stavakavacamālā, coll. and ed. Krishnachandra Gupta and Jyotishacharya Bhrigu. Calcutta: Mahesh Library, n.d.

Śūdraka. *Mṛcchakaṭikam*, ed. R. Dvivedi and J. Vajpeyi. Varanasi: Bharatiya Vidya Prakashan, 1998.

Sūrdās. *Sūrsāgar*, ed. Nandadulare Vajpeyi. 2 vols. Varanasi: Nagari Pracarini Sabha, 1964.

Taittirīyasaṃhitā, ed. A. M. Sastri and K. Rangacharya. Vol. 9. Delhi: Motilal Banarsidass, 1986 [1897].

Tulasīdāsa's Shri Ramacaritamanasa, ed. and tr. R. C. Prasad. Delhi: Motilal Banarsidass, 1999 [1988].

Vālmīki. *Śrīmadvālmikīrāmāyaṇam*. Gorakhpur: Gita Press, Samvat 2056 [1999 C.E.].

Viṣṇusmṛti, ed. K. L. Joshi, tr. M. N. Dutt. Delhi: Parimal Publications, 2006.

Yājñavalkya. *Yājñavalkya Saṃhita: Vyāvahārādhyāyaḥ*, ed. Kumudranjan Ray. Calcutta: K. Ray, 1969.

Yājñavalkya. *Yājñavalkyasmṛti*, ed. Narayan Ram Acharya. Delhi: Nag Publishers, 1985 (reprint, originally published by Nirnay Sagar Press, Bombay).

Secondary sources

Abbott, Justin E. *Bahiṇā Bāī*. Poona: Scottish Mission Industries, 1929.

Archer, W. G. *The Loves of Krishna*. New York: Grove Press, 1960.

Aryan, K. C. *The Little Goddesses (Mātṛkās)*. New Delhi: Rekha Prakashan, 1980.

Bhattacharji, Sukumari. *The Indian Theogony*. Cambridge: Cambridge University Press, 1970.

Bhattacharya, Satyanarayan, ed. *Rāmprasāda Sena: Jivanī o Racanāsamagra*. Calcutta: Book Fair Series, 1975.

Bhattacharya, Sukhamoy Shastri Saptatirtha. *Mahābhāratera Samāja*. Shantiniketan: Visvabharati, 1960.

Bose, Mandakranta, ed. *Faces of the Feminine in Ancient, Medieval and Modern India*. New York: Oxford University Press, 2000.

Brown, C. Mackenzie. *The Triumph of the Goddess*. Albany, NY: State University of New York, 1990.

Bühler, Georg, tr. *The Sacred Laws of the Aryas*. Part 1. Āpastamba and Gautama. 2 vols. Delhi: Motilal Banarsidass, 1992 [1879].

——. *The Sacred Laws of the Aryas*. Part 2. Vasiṣṭha and Baudhāyana. 2 vols. Delhi: Motilal Banarsidass, 1991 [1882].

Chaitanya, Vinaya, tr. *Vacanas of Akka Mahadevi*. Walnut Creek, CA: Altamira Press, 2005.

Chandra, Suresh. *Encyclopaedia of Hindu Gods and Goddesses*. New Delhi: Sarup and Sons, 1998.

Coburn, Thomas. B. *Devī Māhātmya: The Crystalization of the Goddess Tradition*. Delhi: Motilal Banarsidass, 1984.

Dehejia, Vidya, ed. *Āṇṭāl and Her Path of Love*. Albany, NY: State University of New York Press, 1990.

Denton, Lynn Teskey. *Female Ascetics in Hinduism*. Albany, NY: State University of New York Press, 2004.

Doniger O'Flaherty, Wendy. *Hindu Myths*. Harmondsworth: Penguin Books, 1975.

——, tr. *The RigVeda*. London: Penguin Books, 1981.

—— and Brian K. Smith, tr. and annotated. *The Laws of Manu*. London: Penguin Books, 1991.

Embree, Ainslie T. *Sources of Indian Tradition*. Vol. 1. New York: Columbia University Press, 1988.

Flood, Gavin. *An Introduction to Hinduism*. Cambridge: Cambridge University Press, 1996.

Gupta, Sanjukta. *Lakṣmī Tantra: A Pañcarātra Text*. Leiden: E. J. Brill, 1972.

Grierson, George A. and Lionel D. Barnett, eds. *Lāllā-Vākyāni*. London: Royal Asiatic Society, 1920.

Hart, Grorge L. and Hank Heifetz. *The Four Hundred Songs of War and Wisdom*. New York: Columbia University Press, 1999.

Hawley, J. S., ed. *Satī: The Blessings and the Curse*. New York: Oxford University Press, 1994.

—— and Mark Jurgensmeyer, eds. *Songs of the Saints of India*. New York: Oxford University Press, 1988.

Hawley, John S. and D. M. Wulff, eds. *The Divine Consort*. Berkeley, CA: Graduate Theological Union, 1982.

—— and ——, eds. *Devī: Goddesses of India*. Berkeley, CA: University of California Press, 1996.

Hirst, Jacqueline Suthren. *Sītā's Story*. Calgary: Bayeux Arts Inc., 1997.

—— and Lynn Thomas, eds. *Playing for Real: Hindu Role Models, Religion and Gender*. New York: Oxford University Press, 2004.

Ingalls, Daniel H. H. *Sanskrit Poetry*. Cambridge, MA: Harvard University Press, 1979 [1965].

Iyengar, T. R. R. *Dictionary of Hindu Gods and Goddesses*. New Delhi: D.K. Printworld, 2003.

Jackson, William, J. *Vijayanagara Voices*. Burlington, Vt.: Ashgate, 2005.

Jolly, Julius. *Hindu Law and Custom*, tr. Batakrishna Ghosh. Calcutta: Greater India Society, 1928.

——, tr. *The Minor Law Books*. Part 1. Narada and Brihaspati. *Sacred Books of the East*, ed. F. Max Müller, Vol. 33. Delhi: Motilal Banarsidass, 1988 [reprint of Oxford University Press edition, 1889].

Kane, P. V. *History of Dharmashastra*. Vol. 1, pt. 1. Government Oriental Series. Poona: Bhandarkar Oriental Research Institute, 1968.

Keith, A. B. *Veda of the Black Yaju School (Kṛṣṇayajurvedīya Taittirīya Saṃhitā)*. Harvard Oriental Series. Vols. XVIII–XIX. Cambridge, MA: Harvard University Press, 1914.

——. *RigVeda Brāhmaṇas: The Aitareya and Kauṣitakī Brāhmaṇas of the RigVeda*. Harvard Oriental Series. Vol. XXV. Cambridge, MA: Harvard University Press, 1920.

King, Karen L., ed. *Women and Goddess Traditions: In Antiquity and Today*. Minneapolis, MN: Fortress Press, c1997.

Kinsley, David. *The Sword and the Flute. Kālī and Kṛṣṇa: Dark Vision of the Terrible and the Sublime in Hindu Mythology*. Berkeley, CA: University of California Press, 1975.

——. *Hindu Goddesses*. Berkeley, CA: University of California Press, 1986.

——. *The Goddesses' Mirror: Visions of the Divine from East and West*. Albany, NY: State University of New York Press, c1989.

Krishnamachariar, M. *History of Classical Sanskrit Literature*. Delhi: Motilal Banarsidass, 1974 [1937].

Leslie, Julia, ed. *Roles and Rituals for Hindu Women*. Delhi: Motilal Banarsidass, 1992.

——. *The Perfect Wife*, tr. of *Strīdharmapaddhati* by Tryambakayajvan. Delhi: Penguin books, 1995 [1989].

McDermott, Rachel, and Jeffrey Kripal, eds. *Encountering Kālī: In the Margins, At the Center, In the West*. Berkeley, CA: University of California Press, 2003.

Macdonell, A. A. *A Vedic Reader for Students*. Delhi: Oxford University Press, 1993 [1917]

McLean, Malcolm. *Devoted to the Goddess: The Life and Work of Ramprasad*. Albany, NY: State University of New York, 1998.

Menezes, Armando and S. M. Angadi, tr. and ed. *Vacanas of Akka Mahadevi*. Dharwar: Shri Manohar Appasaheb Adke, 1973.

Miller, Barbara Stoler, ed. *Theater of Memory: The Plays of Kālidāsa*. New York: Columbia University Press, 1984.

——. *The Bhagavadgītā*. New York: Bantam Books, 1986.

Monier-Williams, Sir Monier. *A Sanskrit-English Dictionary*. Oxford: Clarendon Press, 1964 [1899].

Mookerjee, Ajit. *Kali: The Feminine Force*. Rochester, VT: Destiny Books, 1988.

Patton, Laurie L., ed. *Jewels of Authority*. New York: Oxford University Press, 2002.

Pauwels, Heidi R. M. *The Goddess as Role Model: Sītā and Rādhā in Scripture and on Screen*. Oxford and New York: Oxford University Press, 2008.

Pillai, S. 'Karaikkal Ammaiyar'. *Women Saints of East and West: Srī Sāradā Devī (the Holy Mother) Birth Centenary Memorial*. London: Ramakrishna Vedanta Centre, 1955.

Pinkham, Mildreth W. *Women in the Sacred Scriptures of Hinduism*. New York: Columbia University Press, 1941.

Pintchman, Tracy. *The Rise of the Goddess in the Hindu Tradition*. Albany, NY: State University of New York, 1994.

Pintchman, Tracy, ed. *Women's Lives, Women's Rituals in the Hindu Tradition*. New York: Oxford University Press, 2007.

Ramanujan, A. K. *Speaking of Śiva*. London: Penguin, 1973.

Ramanujan, A. K. *Poems of Love and War*. New York: Columbia University Press, 1985.

Rhys Davids, C. A. F. and K. R. Norman, tr. *Poems of Early Buddhist Nuns (Therīgāthā)*. Oxford: Pali Text Society, 1989.

Ronan, Stephen. *The Goddess Hekate*. Hastings: Chthonios, 1992.

Ruether, Rosemary Radford. *Goddesses and the Divine Feminine: A Western Religious History*. Berkeley, CA: University of California Press, c2005.

Saraswati, Swami Satyananda. *Kālī Pujā*. Napa, CA: Devi Mandir Publications, 1998 [1996].

Sarkar, Sumit, and Tanika Sarkar, eds., *Women and Social Reform in Modern India: A Reader*. Bloomington, IN: Indiana University Press, c2008.

Sen, Subrata. *The Institution of Strīdhana in the Dharmaśāstra*. Calcutta: Sanskrit College, 1981.

Sharma, Krishna Deo. *Mīrābaī Padāvalī*. Delhi: Regal Book Depot, 1972.

Sircar, D. C., ed. *Foreigners in Ancient India and Lakṣmī and Sarasvatī in Art and Literature*. Calcutta: University of Calcutta, 1970.

Sundaram, P. S., text and tr. *The Poems of Andal: Tiruppavai and Nacciyar Tirumozhi*. Bombay: Ananthacharya Indological Research Institute, 1987.

Tharu, Susie and K. Lalitha, eds. *Women Writing in India: 600* BC *to the Present*. 2 vols. New York: Feminist Press, 1991.

Tiwari, Bhagwandas. *Mīrā kī Prāmānik Padāvalī*. Allahabad: Sahitya Bhavan, 1974.

Tiwari, J. N. *Goddess: Cults in Ancient India*. Delhi: Sundeep Prakashan, 1985.

Vidyavinod, Kalikishore. *Meyedera Vratakathā* [Scripts for Women's *Vratas*]. Calcutta: Akshay Library, 2002.

Articles

Aklujkar, Vidyut. 'Anasūyā: A Pativratā with Panache'. *Faces of the Feminine in Ancient, Medieval and Modern India,* ed. Mandakranta Bose. New York: Oxford University Press, 2000, pp. 36–68.

Behera, K. S. 'Lakṣmī in Orissan Literature and Art'. *Foreigners in Ancient India and Lakṣmī and Sarasvatī in Art and Literature,* ed. D. C. Sircar. Calcutta: University of Calcutta, 1970, pp. 91–105.

Chatterjee, A. K. 'Some Aspects of Sarasvatī'. *Foreigners in Ancient India and Lakṣmī and Sarasvatī in Art and Literature,* ed. D. C. Sircar. Calcutta: University of Calcutta, 1970. pp. 148–53.

Coburn, Thomas. 'Sītā fights while Rāma swoons'. *Mānushī,* no. 90. September–October, 1995, pp. 5–16.

Craddock, Elaine. 'The Anatomy of Devotion: The Life and Poetry of Karaikkal Ammaiyar'. *Women's Lives, Women's Rituals in the Hindu Tradition,* ed. Tracy Pintchman. New York: Oxford University Press, 2007, pp.184–210.

Datta, Krishna. 'A Controversy Over a Verse on the Remarriage of Hindu Women'. *Faces of the Feminine in Ancient, Medieval and Modern India,* ed. Mandakranta Bose. New York: Oxford University Press, 2000, pp. 7–20.

Dev Sen, Nabaneeta. 'Candrāvatī Rāmāyaṇa: Feminizing the Rāma Tale'. *Faces of the Feminine in Ancient, Medieval and Modern India,* ed. Mandakranta Bose. New York: Oxford University Press, 2000, pp. 183–91.

Gupta, Sanjukta Gombrich. 'The Goddess, Women and Their Rituals in Hinduism'. *Faces of the Feminine in Ancient, Medieval and Modern India,* ed. Mandakranta Bose. New York: Oxford University Press, 2000, pp. 87–106.

——. 'Women in Śaiva and Śākta Ethos'. *Roles and Rituals for Hindu Women,* ed. Julia Leslie. Delhi: Motilal Banarsidass, 1992, pp. 193–209.

Jackson, William J. 'Two Poets of the People: Shripadaraya and Atukuri Molla'. *Vijayanagara Voices.* Burlington, VT: Ashgate, 2005, pp. 74–90.

Jamison, Stephanie W. 'Giver or Given: Some Marriages in Kalidāsa'. *Jewels of Authority,* ed. Laurie Patton. New York: Oxford University Press, 2002, pp. 69–83.

Khanna, Madhu. 'The Goddess-Women Equation in Śākta Tantras'. *Faces of the Feminine in Ancient, Medieval and Modern India,* ed. Mandakranta Bose. New York: Oxford University Press, 2000, pp. 109–23.

Kishwar, Madhu. 'Yes to Sita, No to Ram! The Continuing Popularity of Sita in India'. *Manushi,* no. 98, 1997, pp. 21–34.

McDaniel, June. 'Does Tantric Ritual Empower Women? Renunciation and Domesticity among Female Bengali Tantrikas'. *Women's Lives, Women's Rituals in the Hindu Tradition,* ed. Tracy Pintchman. New York: Oxford University Press, 2007, pp. 227–54.

Narayana Rao, Velcheru. 'A *Rāmāyana* of Their Own: Women's Oral Tradition in Telugu'. *Many Rāmāyanas,* ed. Paula Richman. Berkley, CA: University of California Press, 1991, pp. 114–36.

Narayanan, Vasudha. 'The Goddess Śrī: Blossoming Lotus and Breast Jewel of Viṣṇu'. *The Divine Consort,* eds. John S. Hawley and D. M. Wulff. Berkeley, CA: Graduate Theological Union, 1986, pp. 224–37.

O'Flaherty, Wendy Doniger. 'The Shifting Balance of Power in the Marriage of Śiva and Pārvatī'. *The Divine Consort,* eds. John S. Hawley and D. M. Wulff. Berkeley, CA: Graduate Theological Union, 1986, pp. 129–42.

Tripathi, L. K. 'Śrī-Lakṣmī in Early Indian Literature and Art'. *Foreigners in Ancient India and Lakṣmī and Sarasvatiī in Art and Literature,* ed. D. C. Sircar. Calcutta: University of Calcutta, 1970, pp. 158–62.

Index

For Product Safety Concerns and Information please contact our EU
representative GPSR@taylorandfrancis.com
Taylor & Francis Verlag GmbH, Kaufingerstraße 24, 80331 München, Germany

www.ingramcontent.com/pod-product-compliance
Lightning Source LLC
Chambersburg PA
CBHW071517100726
47908CB00004B/1202
9780415620765